M000249977

EMPATH SECRETS

The Ultimate Guide for Empaths and Highly Sensitive People to Shield Yourself From Negative Energies, Manage Your Empathy and Develop Your Gift.

|Life Strategies for Sensitive People|

| *May 2021 Edition*|

Table Of Contents

Introduction...7

The Empathy Scale 7

Chapter 1 What is empath? **10**

Definition of an Empath: 10

Finding the Answers to Who you are: 13

Chapter 2 Empath Types...**36**

Emotional Empaths.. 37

   Emotional Empaths as Healers 39

Physical Empaths... 41

   Physical Empaths as Healers 41

Synesthetic Empaths 43

   Synesthetic Empaths as Healers...................................... 44

Animal Empaths 45

   Animal Empaths as Healers 46

Plant Empaths.. 46

   Plant Empaths as Healers.. 47

Geomantic Empaths 48

   Geomantic Empaths as Healers.. 49

Rare Empath types.. 50

   Intuitive Empaths (also called Claircognizant Empaths)...................... 51

Chapter 3 How to Know If You are an Empath **56**

Chapter 4 Empaths, emotions, and health: How to stop absorbing other people's distress **62**

The Science of Empathy *64*

The Evolutionary Purpose of Empathy *66*

Empathy vs. Empathic Sensitivity *67*

Common Traits of an Empath *69*

The Empath and the Highly Sensitive Person *70*

Chapter 5 Empaths, love, and sex **73**

Sabotaging Your Relationships *81*

Compromising the boundaries 81

Express your needs 82

Not sharing 83

A parent-child relationship 84

Balance Being An Empath *84*

Assessing your emotions 86

Being okay 86

Don't keep saying yes 87

Time to unplug 88

Stop seeking validation 88

Chapter 6 Empaths and Work **90**

Always Ask For A Workplace Tour Before Accepting A Role *99*

Use Your Gift As A Selling Point *100*

Working Alone Versus Working With Others *101*

If Your Environment Drains Your Energy, Ask For Reasonable Adjustments *102*

Watch Out For Energy Vampires... 103

Draw A Line Between Your Workplace and Home 104

Focus On How Your Work Helps Others... 105

Chapter 7 Increase the effects of communication with people 107

Am I Paying Full Attention?... 107

Are Your Multi-Tasking? 108

Did You Ever Check How Your Actions Are Affecting the Person in Front of You? 109

Are Your Listening with the Intent to Understand?................................ 110

Chapter 8 Techniques of improve your persuasion skills even if you are a beginner..**113**

Say Thanks for The Things You Have... 113

Learn to Accept... 114

Keep Your Mind on the Right Track 115

Make Amends 116

Be Kind 117

Clean Your Home... 118

Mix with the Right Kind of People... 118

Get Exposed to the Right Kind of Media.. 119

Validate Yourself... 120

Chapter 9 Application in the Real World...............................**123**

Conclusion...**131**

Legal & Disclaimer

The information contained in this book and its contents is not designed to replace or take the place of any form of medical or professional advice; and is not meant to replace the need for independent medical, financial, legal or other professional advice or services, as may be required. The content and information in this book has been provided for educational and entertainment purposes only.

The content and information contained in this book has been compiled from sources deemed reliable, and it is accurate to the best of the Author's knowledge, information and belief. However, the Author cannot guarantee its accuracy and validity and cannot be held liable for any errors and/or omissions. Further, changes are periodically made to this book as and when needed. Where appropriate and/or necessary, you must consult a professional (including but not limited to your doctor, attorney, financial advisor or such other professional advisor) before using any of the suggested remedies, techniques, or information in this book.

Upon using the contents and information contained in this book, you agree to hold harmless the Author from and against any damages, costs, and expenses, including any legal fees potentially resulting from the application of any of the information provided by this book. This disclaimer applies to any loss, damages or injury caused by the use and application, whether directly or indirectly, of any advice or information presented, whether for breach of contract, tort, negligence, personal injury, criminal intent, or under any other cause of action.

You agree to accept all risks of using the information presented inside this book.

You agree that by continuing to read this book, where appropriate and/or necessary, you shall consult a professional (including but not limited to your doctor, attorney, or financial advisor or such other advisor as needed) before using any of the suggested remedies, techniques, or information in this book.

Introduction

In order to understand why empaths are so well suited to the healing arts, we must first look at their most common characteristics, and examine the ways in which the empath typically differs from the average individual. We'll also clarify the definition of empathy as a fluid, rather than fixed, trait, which can be both good and bad, rather than the exemplary moral virtue it is often believed to be.

The Empathy Scale

Many of us fall into the habit of describing empathy as a personality trait that people either have in spades or lack entirely. It does simplify things when we look at the personalities of others as innate, fixed, and predictable, allowing us to praise and embrace those we think of as warm and giving, while we can write off those we see as callous or self-absorbed.

In truth, though, empathy is one of several "traits" that would be better described as "skills." While the scientific analysis does show evidence that some degree of empathetic capacity stems from genetic inheritance, there is far more evidence to show that empathy is either fostered or repressed experientially in most individuals. Empathy is not something you are born with or born without—instead, it is a coping mechanism that most all of us rely on in early life. Our childhood surroundings will often determine the extent to which we continue to rely on empathy for survival, as we grow to adulthood, or learn to loosen its grip on our emotional and physical bodies so that we can function as individuals.

Most people learn, as they mature, to fall somewhere in the middle of the empathy scale; from this position, they are able to connect empathetically with those they love, or sometimes with strangers, when they have the capacity and strength to do so, while disconnecting from their empathic impulses when it makes more sense to focus on their own feelings and needs. These people are able to give to charities without bankrupting themselves; they are also able to support their friends emotionally, but avoid those who are suffering when they need to focus on their own emotional pain. This is considered the "normal" range of empathy.

Things work differently on the far ends of the empathy scale, though. Some of us may learn to detach from our empathetic impulses entirely, developing empathy-deficient personality disorders (such as antisocial personality disorder or narcissistic personality disorder, among others); meanwhile, there are some who grow up in environments that never train them to manage their empathetic impulses, whose emotional behavior might be described as "hyper-empathetic." Those who are empathy-deficient will often present as self-absorbed, inconsiderate, greedy or stingy, and uncaring; they might never feel compelled to donate a penny to charity, despite having more money than they could ever feasibly spend in their own lifetime. Meanwhile, empaths, or hyper-empathetic people, tend to be far more focused on others than on themselves; they can be overly generous, highly sensitive, deeply affectionate, compassionate, and selfless, often to a fault.

The impulse to empathize with others may be naturally stronger in some people than others, but regardless of the person's background and current persona, their empathetic capacity can always be enhanced, or grow more inaccessible through lack of use. Empathy is quite a bit like muscle mass; anyone can lose their empathetic strength through prolonged emotional laziness or by embracing a defensive mindset, but at the same time, there's nothing to stop even the leanest and weakest among us from growing strong and powerful, so long as they are willing to do some hard, transformative work and break their counterproductive habits.

Chapter 1 What is empath?

The word empath refers to someone who feels the emotions of another person as their own feelings. For instance, an empath may begin feeling mad because there is someone mad around them at the time.

Growing Numbers:

A higher number of individuals claim to have this experience in their daily lives and it usually happens without an awareness of the process.

Definition of an Empath:

What exactly does the term "empath" mean? It refers to having the ability to sense the emotions of other people and to some may sound like a fictional super power.

The number continues to grow of people claiming to have unusual emotional experiences, often seeming to happen despite their input or control.

How this Term becomes Known:

Though some people will hear this term from a practitioner of alternative medicine or a friend, a lot of people are just looking for the key to their unexplainable personality.

Eventually, with some patience and time, these individuals will find the word "empath." Searching on the internet for this term used to only show websites that said this ability wasn't real, but the trend has grown within the last decade as people have shared their real experiences in life.

Finding valuable Information:

Of course, some of these websites are only looking to sell services and products to the people seeking truth, but there is plenty of valuable information given by those who understand what it's like and want to help other empaths.

Reading about the Experience is the First Step:

Just having the ability to research and connect with others who understand is very validating for the beginner empath who has finally realized that they aren't alone or crazy.

Continuing research and finding tools for getting the most out of life as an empath will pay off and is a great place to start on this path.

Anyone can be an Empath: Looking through some posts online by self-proclaimed empaths will show you that this trait can belong to anyone, including real estate agents, engineers, and nurses.

Of course, not all of these people will recognize or even accept that this is what they are.

Mental Troubles: We will discuss more about the challenges of empaths throughout the book, but for now suffice it to say that depression and anxiety are rampant in the community of empaths.

They will often readily admit that they have suffered intensely both psychologically and emotionally because of their gift, which can feel more like a curse, at times.

It isn't just the process of feeling negative emotions, but dealing with acceptance of their personality, rather than denial or the firm belief that it's impossible.

You're not Crazy:

Sadly, most empaths don't know what is going on with them or what they're experiencing. They think that their feelings either aren't real or that others feel the same way they feel.

It isn't a topic that many feel ready to talk to friends or family about, meaning that the confusion can last for a long time.

Shame and Ridicule:

Actually, children who have attempted to explain their experiences have often been labeled as too sensitive, weird, or imagining things.

But this isn't something that an empath can turn off at will, regardless of how hard they try to do so. This will lead them to return to the question again and again of whether they can really feel others' emotions or whether they are just crazy.

Seeking the Answers:

People who discuss sensing others' emotions are not just crazy. They know that this is not considered possible by most people in modern society and spend a huge amount of energy and time trying to look for answers before they find the term "empath."

Trying to find Relief:

Empaths try to find relief in their own way, even if it isn't always healthy. Many of them have tried alcohol, drugs, medications, and therapy to escape from their difficult mental and emotional symptoms.

But eventually, avoidance doesn't work anymore and the mind becomes open to other explanations and possibilities. Eventually, denial no longer works and you are only left with the truth of your situation.

Finding the Answers to Who you are:

Many times, even as they wonder whether they're delusional, empaths notice that they are different than others. They sense this from a very young age and it never goes away.

How do they Find the Answer?

Often, it comes down to hearing the description from someone else (usually on the internet) that leads the empath to finally have a glimpse of recognition.

Recognizing Symptoms: They see themselves in the symptoms listed, like hating crowds, feeling the world as something heavy, and getting easily overwhelmed by emotional conversations.

Empaths also report that they feel emotions in a physical way, including vertigo, nausea, or a knotted stomach for no discernible physical reason. These are all common, everyday situations for the average empath.

Eliminating Coincidence: Eventually, the explanation of coincidence is no longer satisfactory. The empath starts to realize the link between the feeling they had and the proximity of another person feeling emotional stress.

An empath will often feel nauseous walking by a busy mall because of all the people inside feeling a mix of emotions. They don't like to be near crowds all the time because it's difficult for them.

In addition to this, they might describe how anxious they got listening to someone talking about their emotional difficulties, feeling the suffering as their own suffering.

And usually, there's a certain event that makes obvious the connection between their emotional experience and someone else's feelings.

Biological Processes: There are some fascinating biological components in the process of emotional experience. When you sense a feeling, there is also a complex series of physical processes happening alongside them.

This points to the biological basis for why empaths exist.

There are many theories around the concept of empaths. Some even think that the concept of the empath is completely made up! Others believe that empaths have special psychic abilities.

Let's explore that idea first and then we'll go over some of the other common beliefs about empaths.

Theories about the Empath's Psychic Abilities:

Psychic people usually can tell that they are not like others in indefinable ways. Although it's generally accepted in the psychic community that most people possess at least partial psychic abilities, some have them more than others.

This is because of differing biological predispositions. Those who possess psychic abilities were always born with them.

Psychic ability comes from a bigger process that includes sensitivity to emotions and the environment.

Females and High Empathy:

Psychic ability seems to arise from the right side of the brain. Female brains are less one sided and more lateralized than most male brains, so it shouldn't be much of a surprise that most psychic people (and empaths) are female.

Empathy and Right Brain Dominance:

Some believe that heightened empathy (like those experienced by the empath personality type) is a type of psychic ability.

A right-brain dominant person will often experience different patterns of thought than other people, including higher than average creative thinking and holistic reasoning.

Physical Differences in Empaths and Psychics:

The intensity of right brain dominance depends on individual degree and the people who fall into this category will have different ways of thinking than the average person.

To put it another way, there are physical reasons why empaths and psychic people strongly feel that they are different.

The Vulnerabilities of Highly Sensitive Empaths:

Psychics are also called ASP (anomalously sensitive people). This is because their sensitivities stretch beyond sensing the emotions of others.

In what other ways are they different?

Allergies and Sickness: Physical sensitivities exist for them such as sensitivities to substances and over-active immune functions. Along with this there are overload and aesthetic sensitivities.

In general, these types are more vulnerable in terms of autoimmune diseases and allergies.

Self-Healing Ability: But in addition to getting sick easier, the highly sensitive empath is best suited for self-healing and can use their strong intention to reduce stress and negative influence in their lives.

They can bring the placebo effect to live instead of pretending that it's real, convincing their mind and body to follow the belief.

Intuitive and Introverted types: This type of sensitivity impacts emotions and is associated highly with emotional intuition and sensitivity.

Feeling, intuitive, and introverted are often all qualities of empaths.

They are intuitive because they use their feelings to respond to information and introverted because they get easily overwhelmed when exposed to the strong emotions of others.

As you can see, this is a special power to have, but it doesn't always feel that way and won't until you learn how to use the gift in a healthy way. This book is a great place to start for learning how.

In this chapter, we will talk about the possible biological processes that make and shape the experience of the empath, like their mirror neurons.

It will also talk about the experience of the empath versus the concept of empathy itself, and the common struggles empaths face on a daily basis, like a lack of good information, fear of ridicule, and even mental illness.

We will finally go over the innate, deeper purpose for this ability and valuable tools for making it a gift instead of a curse.

Theories related to Empaths:

Empaths often experience the feelings of other people as though they are their own feelings.

Initially seen in science fiction movies and novels, this idea has grown in popularity as more and more people identify with this trait.

The internet is now full of people who vehemently state that this is not just fiction but reality and anyone who has empath tendencies knows that the phenomenon is all too real.

Mirror Neurons:

Some believe that the empath ability is related to high functioning or over-active mirror neurons. Some things can appear to be magical until the processes involved are fully understood.

A New and Undeveloped Study:

For the average empath, unfortunately, this process of discovery is currently in progress. But scientific study of mirror neurons can help us understand why empaths feel others' emotions and what the experience is like for them.

One can hope that we will soon live in a world where this ability is not ridiculed. How are mirror neurons related to heightened empathy?

What are Mirror Neurons?

Mirror neurons are a neurophysiological process that helps us both understand and imitate the actions of other people. They were first discovered in relation to motor skills that fired up in a monkey's brain when it was watching someone do something.

This discovery lead to an idea that observing people doing an action leads to a response I our brains that aid us in copying what we are observing.

Just watching someone else experience something activates these neurons in us, even if we don't make a single movement.

The Basis for Morality and Empathy:

This is where the link between mirror neurons and empathy becomes clear. In Marco Iacoboni's book, "Mirroring People," the author talks about the way this new research has developed.

He brings up mirror neurons as a possible explanation for morality and empathy. This is because they appear to be related to the way we observe, perceive, and ultimately interpret others' experiences.

An Internal Reaction to Stimuli:

A mirror neuron can be simply explained as being triggered by watching a physical action in another person, which then fires off the same neurons in the person watching the action.

The fascinating thing about this function is that it will consistently occur even when the observer isn't moving at all. The mirroring doesn't involve physical imitation, but just forms a representation internally.

This can explain why we are so fascinated and interested in sports, for instance.

The neurons that fire off when the player catches a ball will also fire off in the audience members' brains as they observe this action.

How this relates to Emotions:

This process is working, as well, when we observe a person showing signs of worry or anger, or experiencing some kind of pain on a physical level.

This allows our brains to interpret what these situations mean by letting us experience them in our own minds.

There are many different ways for mirror neurons to get triggered, from watching someone ick a ball, to hearing the sound of someone kicking a ball, or even just someone speaking the word "kick" out loud.

A Survival-related Function of the Brain:

When our mirror neurons fire off, the pattern is so complex that we are able to use it to understand what someone's intentions or thoughts are, in relation to the action they have performed.

The existence of this mental process is crucial in terms of relating to people and understanding them, both of which are necessary for the survival of our species. This idea is supported, as well, by another subject of study known as emotional contagion.

What is Emotional Contagion and How does it Relate to Empaths?

Emotional contagion happens when a group or person influences the actions of another group or person. This can be done either consciously or unconsciously and is performed through inducing behaviors and emotional states.

Some may say that empaths simply have a far more advanced ability for this, but as stated before, research on the phenomenon of empaths is still new and much is yet to be determined.

A Natural Human Ability: Although empaths may have a higher proclivity for this, the process of emotional contagion is rooted very deeply within the psyche of human nature.

Even newborn babies can imitate other people's facial expressions mere moments after they are born.

Unconscious Imitation: When we grow up, we also copy others' demeanor, often without realizing we are doing it. This type of mimicry spreads feelings from one individual to another and plays a big role in human social relationships.

Actually, it's a fact that humans are more likely to feel favorably towards those who copy their actions (subtly, of course).

The Purpose of Emotional Contagion: It's believed that this mimicry lets us connect with others on a deeper level, providing us with a positive feeling state.

The process of emotional contagion grows from simple mimicry when we wish to feel loved by and close to other people. The ability to connect to other people is a necessity for the survival of the human race and we attempt to copy nonverbal cues from babyhood and childhood on.

If it's true that an empath simply has a heightened ability for this function, it would seem like this has a purpose for the survival of our species, as well.

Science hasn't advanced quite this far yet, but the experience of the empath appears to show that there's a way for humans to sense others' emotions instantly and innately.

This is outside of their conscious reasoning.

Many struggling empaths would switch this process off if they could and make it so that their emotions were the only ones they felt.

But the experience of being an empath always starts uncontrollably and unconsciously.

Just as emotional contagion and mirror neurons activate without us choosing so, empaths report that they soak up the emotions of others without wanting or trying to.

Developing the Empath Skill in a Conscious Way:

The skill of high empathy is not comparable to other skills. With most interest or skills, you have to consciously choose to acquire them.

Typical Skill-Building: Most often, when someone wishes to grow or expand one of their skills, like kicking a ball for instance, you first have to decide to do this, and then begin to practice faithfully.

Some are going to be naturally more skilled than other people with some pursuits and may not need as much practice.

However, there's always a natural progression from the choice to learn a skill to the physical choice to make it happen (by practicing).

The Empath Skill: For empaths, however, the physical skill arrives first. They will soak up other people's feelings without choosing to do so or without even realizing that it's happening.

Only after going through the question of figuring out how to stop it do they finally realize that it can't be turned off and they must embark on a journey to truly understand themselves and how they fit into this world.

For empaths, the skill lies in learning how to consciously wield their ability.

Feeling First: The experience of being an empath is not something that you learn or something that a child could hope to have and practice until they get it.

The original trigger for this appears to be something physical (like feeling an emotion's sensation), which results in an experience on an emotional level, then the cognition and awareness of it.

Essentially, the empath will feel first and then hopefully understand what they felt later on.

A Lack of Control: In addition, most empaths report that they cannot control this process of sensing emotion. This is yet another piece of the puzzle that appears to make high empathy a natural ability.

But not every person reports being able to sense the emotions of those around them. On the other hand, only a tiny percentage of people even consider that this is possible.

Even though everyone can perceive the emotions of others (with a few exceptions), the empath appears to have a very high sensitivity to cues of emotion and feeling states.

Are Empaths just "Sensitive"?

The idea of innate sensitivity is foundational to the experience of the empath. Empaths usually report feeling moved by reading or watching something, like a disturbing or sad book or movie.

They may even avoid watching news programs since just listening to someone describe a disaster can cause them overwhelming distress.

An empath can listen to their friend talk about something stressful and still feel that negative feeling hours later.

Since negative feelings are more noticeable and salient, a lot of empaths feel weighed down by the world.

Labeled as Sensitive: Empaths are very often said to be sensitive, both through the observation of those close to them and their own self-reasoning.

Perhaps that isn't very surprising when you consider that they always feel something, be it other people's emotions or their own.

They are being activated emotionally on a nearly constant basis which can make them seem too sensitive.

The Sensitive Nervous System: But it might be more than just an emotional way of being. Empaths may have a more sensitive nervous system than other people.

Studies have shown that some individuals are physically more sensitive than the average person. Even infants show different reactions to unfamiliar stimuli.

One study showed that of nearly 500 participants studied, about 20 percent of them reacted more intensely to tactile, auditory, and visual stimulations.

Understanding High Sensitivity:

The idea of a highly sensitive person is appropriate for those who react intensely to the situations of life.

Some even believe that sensitivity is a trait of personality that is more complicated than the extroverted/introverted concepts of Jungian psychology.

The Overwhelming World: Certain people are born sensitive and have a harder time feeling comfortable with life. Our minds and bodies will always look for a happy center point between over stimulation and boredom.

When you're very sensitive, the world feels overwhelming. Everything from strong odors and colors, to loud noises and bright lights can lead to an overstressed state of mind for the empath.

Sensitivity as a Gift: Being sensitive in this way is a talent, skill, and gift that must be appreciated and praised, rather than ridiculed and criticized.

Once empaths and highly sensitive folks understand the reasons behind their reactions, life will make sense. They will finally come to a place of self-acceptance and learn to thrive as who they really are.

This is a huge step up from the ideas of "something must be wrong with me" that many empaths grow up dealing with.

Many of the struggles that highly sensitive people and empaths deal with in life, from not being understood by parents to struggling to relate to friends, can be explained by their nervous system.

Just as some naturally have higher than average vision or hearing, empaths likely have a stronger ability to sense emotional signals.

Sending and Receiving Signals:

There is one aspect to the experience of being an empath that is hard for people to wrap their heads around and that is empaths perceiving emotions of other people who are not physically near them.

Empaths say that they feel the emotions of friends and family, even when those people live very far away.

Is this Possible? This may sound unbelievable on the surface, but the explanation could be simpler than it sounds.

If certain emotions trigger pathways in our neurons, the field that its electrical activity generates could be sensed by another person's mirror neurons, resulting in emotional contagion.

If you consider one person being the sender and the other person being a receiver, both of the people involved have the equipment need to both pickup and send emotional signals.

Sensing Fields of Emotion: The first person could be automatically sending a field that has information about their emotional state within it, similar to the way MRI scans can reflect the brain's internal activities.

The second person could then get and read this signal with their neurons, picking up on the other person's feelings.

Unlike electrical currents, magnetic waves are able to travel very far and go through solid material.

The ability to sense these fields is debated and considered controversial, but it's a theory for why empaths can sense others' emotions from far away.

What would be needed for that to Happen?

What would be necessary for that to be possible? The first person would need to have an emotion that is specific and strong enough to be both send and interpreted by the second person.

This idea is consistent with what empaths experience, which involves getting overwhelmed by feelings like depression and danger.

Empaths also often state that the feeling they soak up from another person will remain with them for longer periods if it's a very strong emotion.

Secondly, the other person would need to have a strong sensitivity to be able to pick up on the field being transmitted and interpret what it means.

This is another area in which empaths are very different from the average person.

In daily life, they get described as being too sensitive, which just mean experiencing emotions on a deep, constant basis.

In the hypothetical scenario we're discussing, the second person would need to be sensitive enough to tell the emotional signal apart from other signals, and also know how to tell what the emotion they are feeling is (such as happiness or sadness).

This indicates a specialized skill.

Possible Psychological Reasons for the Empath:

Empathy is an idea that is talked about in psychology and described as imagining how another person feels. This ability plays a huge role in social situations.

Having empathy for other people can change the way we interact with that person. Empath may, for instance, make us hug a person who is feeling upset.

This ability is a crucial aspect of what makes society possible for us.

Though people, like sociopaths, who suffer from some psychopathologies, show an absence of empathy, they are a rare exception.

As mentioned earlier, infants are able to recognize various emotions from a very early age and young children grow in their ability for empathy the older they get.

Kids can tell what another person is feeling and respond appropriately, by offering comfort when it's necessary. Empathy is knowing how to perceive the internal state of another accurately and to imagine it's happening to us.

Some believe that empathy is a process involving imagining the emotions of other people. For the empath, however, it feels like anything but imagination.

Empaths and Spirituality:

Empaths can go nearly their whole lives without realizing that they are an empath. They may assume that all people feel the world in the same way that they do.

Only when they get older do they realize that they are different.

They will seek out solutions and answers, for many years sometimes, without finding what they are looking for.

It can be a great relief to learn about the term "empath" and it usually occurs accidentally.

Regardless of how one discovers their true nature, self-awareness will always be a challenge for the empath since their personality type is still such a mystery.

Feeling Ashamed: Different empaths will experience their gift in different ways, which can make defining the empath even harder.

Even when an empath recognizes that someone else might share their trait, they may have a hard time knowing how to bring it up in conversation.

Since the word itself is associated with science fiction and fantasy, it makes it even harder for people to admit what they are experiencing.

They feel a sense of shame or fear of judgment for who they are.

Turning Points or Triggers: Some empath types say that a specific situation or event is what caused their abilities to awaken, like a pregnancy, sudden sickness, or car accident.

Some of these occurrences could be traumatic, while others seem neutral or even positive. However, each of these events appeared to be a new level for them that led them to stop denying their innate abilities.

Oftentimes, the triggering event first leads to a denial phase or difficulty accepting what is happening.

Being Born with the Ability: There is also the other case of people who felt as though they were born with their skill. One major difference between these types is an understanding relative who may have brought it up to them at a young age.

When an empath has someone like this around, it appears to have a dramatic impact on how much the empath will accept their skill and develop their abilities.

They will also be more likely to have a strong state of mind.

Empaths tend to thrive when they have a positive attitude about their personality. This proves that even for those who have struggled with accepting themselves, changes can be made for the better.

A Trait without Choice: Regardless of how the skill comes to be known, most empaths don't feel like they chose what they have. Most empaths feel like they were forced to be this way and see it as something undesirable or inevitable.

This personality type does not happen by choice.

Seeking Purpose as an Empath:

One common question asked by empaths is "What is the reason for this?"

Even though each person has a different person reason, there is one common theme within the experience of the empath that lends spiritual meaning to it and that is its direct contact with humanity and consciousness.

A Natural Need: From childhood on, humans seek out connection to their fellow humans. As much as some of us might like to be, the human race is not solitary, but highly social.

From friends to parents, we dedicate a huge portion of our lives to pursuing connected and meaningful relations with others. But forming these valuable connections is a challenge.

Just a quick Google search on the topic will show you how hard it is to authentically communicate with others.

A Lack of Authenticity: This trouble connecting is especially common in the modern world where many of the accepted social conventions discourage genuine interaction.

For instance, pretending to like someone in order to appear polite or hiding your anger because it isn't nice or feminine.

There are plenty of reasons why individuals keep their feelings hidden, which has given us the difficult situation of wanting to relate to others but not being able to tell how they are really feeling.

Authenticity seems to have been weeded from our nature.

Disconnecting from our emotions is not natural and leads us to suffer as we suppress them out of fear. We get pushed ever farther away from genuine connection and pushed closer to social obligation or fakeness.

As social beings, not having this need to connect deeply leaves us feeling malnourished emotionally. And most of us have even forgotten how to go beyond this problem.

The Necessity for Empaths: Looking at this situation, perhaps it's not very surprising that empaths have evolved within our society. They bring something that many others have lost; the ability to read others' emotions in a true and genuine way.

They can read another person's emotions, even without nonverbal or verbal cues. They are able to connect with what is most genuine inside of another person.

Most humans are disconnected from nature these days, but regardless of that, nature impacts them and strives to keep them balanced.

Life strives to find balance regardless of how much humans disregard it. The empath is a manifestation of something drastically different than the norm of being emotionally disconnected.

It could be nature's attempt to redistribute itself in a way that makes more sense. The average modern human struggles deeply with talking about their emotions.

They might feel drawn to the empath inexplicably because they can sense that the empath can feel what they feel.

The Empath's Purpose of Healing and Opening:

Empaths have a reflex to heal and take away pain from other people, and they don't choose this reflex. It's as natural as needing water to survive.

Even when they might prefer to run away and hide from the difficulty, they can't help but stay and try to help.

In addition to this, they might feel that there's a deeper reason why they have this tendency. They might feel that their experience is helping to open up a blocked passage that must be released.

Even though they often have a hard time putting words to the phenomenon, most empaths can sense their healing powers.

Simply knowing how another feels does not magically heal it, but it can present a chance to have a more genuine talk about emotion.

Chapter 2 Empath Types

o two empaths are created equal. While most of the available literature on empaths and empath healing tend to focus on the experience of emotional empaths, there are those whose empathetic sensitivity is focused more on physical rather than emotional sensations. There are some who struggle to connect emotionally with most humans, but can easily empathize with animals, plants, or non-living entities, such as places, rocks, or even metaphysical concepts. Some are able to connect with energetic frequencies that are far removed from their present circumstances, rooted in the past, the future, or alternative planes of existence.

Below, we'll explore the most common categorical empath types. As you read, be mindful of the fact that there are always further possibilities; some empaths identify as a combination of two or more types, while some never find a categorical title that seems to fit their specific empathic experience. If you do find that one or more of the type descriptions below strikes a familiar chord, consider this typology as merely a jumping-off point for further research and connection with similar empaths. Don't allow any type to limit your perceptions or belief in your own powers. Many empaths find that their abilities expand and intensify as they age and develop more emotional and spiritual maturity; if you identify as an animal empath now, there is no reason why you might not evolve into an emotional empath at a later point in time. Always keep yourself open to the possibility of growth.

Emotional Empaths

Of all the empath types, emotional empaths are by far the most common. This is perhaps because emotional empathy is a skill most of us already possess in infancy; while many outgrow these strong empathic connections and learn to numb themselves to the emotional energies around them, a fair number of us hold onto this ability in adulthood, and some are even able to train and strengthen their sensitivity to emotional vibrations as they grow older. Some emotional empaths learn to stifle their emotional instincts in adolescence when they begin to learn that others see their sensitivity as a weakness or an annoyance, but most often their empathic gifts will come back to them with an explosive degree of force at some point later in life. Often, emotional empaths rediscover their true identities during the dissolution of a toxic relationship, whether it is familial, professional, platonic, or romantic.

Most emotional empaths feel strong emotional connections to those who are in close proximity to them—strangers they pass by on a walk through the park, for instance—but some are more sensitive to the emotions of people they care for, regardless of how much distance may lay between them. Emotional empaths often pick up on energetic frequencies that vibrate between people, meaning they are able to understand the nuances of others' relationships and detect subtle energetic shifts in group dynamics. They also note tensions between others, however subtle, whether it is sexual tension or the uncomfortable energy created by anger or resentment.

Many emotional empaths can also feel it in their bodies when someone has told a lie, even if the lie wasn't delivered directly to them. As an example, an emotional empath might show up to a birthday party and see a group of friends they haven't interacted with for months; one of the guests at this party has been cheating on their partner, who is also present, for several weeks, and another guest knows about the infidelity, so the two of them have had to tell a number of white lies and greater lies in order to keep this secret under wraps. Even before the empath interacts with either of these people, they are very likely to feel, immediately upon arriving at the party, that something isn't right. They may not know what exactly is causing this negative energy straight away, but as the party continues, they will likely be able to pinpoint where the negative energy is coming from or to sense that the nature of this energy is dishonesty or betrayal.

Empaths are especially sensitive to lies that are told directly to their faces and usually know immediately, down to their bones, when someone has been dishonest with them. This being the case, many emotional empaths have social lives that appear complicated or disjointed to the outside observer. Lies and emotional abuse between other people literally hurt them, so empowered empaths with firm boundaries often know that it's best to walk away from social circles that tolerate or encourage such dynamics. Of all the empath types, emotional empaths are perhaps the most susceptible to narcissistic abuse or exploitation from energy vampires.

Emotional Empaths as Healers

Emotional empaths tend to find their stride as healers of emotional wounds. They are particularly skilled at guiding others through trauma recovery, personal evolution, and release of false psychological complexes. They may also naturally drift into the repair—or dismantling—of unhealthy relationships and toxic cycles, like emotional abuse. Many choose to work as therapists or counselors for individuals, couples, or families, but this work can be quite draining for them. Others may find they are better able to help people through writing, public speaking, or artistic creativity, as these fields allow them to reach a large number of people without leaving themselves constantly vulnerable to emotional contagion, burnout, and compassion fatigue.

Emotional empaths can also apply their skills to the world of medical healing, though this choice is less common. The medical field seldom gives weight to the impact that our emotional bodies can have on our physical ones and vice versa; so, while emotional empaths may be apter than non-empathic medical professionals at untangling complicated diagnoses or understanding the roots of physical pain and other symptoms, their empathic knowledge will usually need to be translated or disguised in some way in order for the empath to be taken seriously. For instance, an emotional empath working as a pediatrician might sense that a child's chronic skin rash has a root in an emotional disturbance— perhaps an authority figure in the child's life is taking advantage of their position and abusing them, either emotionally or physically—but this empath would not be able to tell the child's parents, or their colleagues, that they believe the rash is merely a symptom of holding in a secret that the child thinks of as shameful. They could not send the parents away with a recommended course of radical honesty as a treatment. Their insight may prove quite valuable, but will only be respected if they are able to couch their knowledge within a more widely recognized framework.

Furthermore, emotional empaths can be extraordinarily valuable in the world of physical medicine because they will ensure patients are offered compassion and emotional comfort during treatment. Many doctors lack empathy, at least during work hours, as a way to protect themselves from grief; if they allow themselves to care about their patients, they run the risk of being heartbroken when they are unable to save them from their own mortalities. They aim to care for the patient's body as though it were detached from the soul and mind inside it. By contrast, the emotional empath as a nurse or doctor is far more likely to recognize the importance of good mental and emotional health in any patient's recovery process, and prioritize things like family or friend visits, good nutritional health, books and games to keep the mind active, exposure to sunlight and nature, and so on. They will recognize their patients as whole beings, with a body, mind, and soul all intertwined in such a way that none can function without the other two in balance. They can also have an enormous impact on the lives of those who love their patients, simply by delivering diagnoses or difficult news with compassion in place of impassivity.

Physical Empaths

Physical empaths (also called "medical empaths") are somewhat less common than emotional empaths, though a great number of empaths identify with both types simultaneously. The strictly physical empath is more attuned to the physical experiences of others than their emotional sensations. Some claim they can literally feel the pleasure or pain experienced in another person's body, while others can see or otherwise detect physical disturbances in the energy fields of others. Some might see injuries or illnesses in others' bodies as a color shift in their aura, for example, while some might detect physical ailments through other senses instead, like smell or touch.

Physical Empaths as Healers

Physical empaths are often naturally gifted at hands-on healing practices, such as massage, acupressure, acupuncture, reflexology, chiropractic alignment, yoga instruction, physical therapy, and even traditional western medicine. They have a keen ability to pinpoint the source of another's pain or the root of an illness and can understand physical sensations that patients struggle to describe with language.

The physical empath who chooses to apply their gifts to healing work must stay vigilant in order to protect their own physical body. While they may find they are extraordinarily efficient and talented in whatever healing art they choose, able to secure diagnoses and prescribe treatment much more quickly than their non-empathic counterparts, they may also soon discover that healing work, unfortunately, leaves them quite vulnerable to contracting illnesses and chronic pain disorders themselves. It is not at all uncommon for physical empath healers to report that they experience the full range of painful or uncomfortable sensations that their patients complain of, sometimes retaining these symptoms long after their patients are cured or relieved.

Sadly, physical empaths who suffer from this type of contagion will find it frustrating and difficult to get their own maladies diagnosed or treated by doctors of western medicine, who may infer that their pain or illness is all psychosomatic. It is recommended that physical empath healers rely heavily on their own trusted energy healers to help them maintain metaphysical boundaries, heal imbalances, and untangle their personal bodily feelings from those of their patients and clients. It is also recommended that physical empaths avoid overworking themselves, and aim to work in environments where they can focus on one client at a time without being rushed. A physical empath working in a busy clinic, for instance, or in a chaotic emergency ward, will likely struggle to maintain their energetic boundaries and adequately protect themselves.

Synesthetic Empaths

Synesthesia is a fairly rare condition, though it is widely recognized in medical and scientific fields, wherein a person's perceptions of sensory experiences are confused, tangled, or enmeshed. For instance, there are synesthetes who claim to hear colors, feel numerical values, or taste sounds; others might only be able to make sense of the information they see and hear when they have access to both audio and visual stimulus together; some even incorporate extrasensory knowledge, assigning emotional values to things like flavors, colors, or specific notes on the musical scale, perhaps even personifying non-living entities. Not all synesthetes are empaths, but those who are can often access levels of empathic knowledge and sensitivity that mystify the rest of the world, even other powerful and experienced empaths.

Mirror-touch synesthesia is a rare condition to find in the general populace, but it is a particularly common type of synesthesia amongst empaths, in which the visual and tactile cues are mixed up in the brain. An empath with mirror-touch synesthesia could witness another person being pinched on the forearm, and feel pain in their own arm as a result. Likewise, they could witness another person being hugged, and feel the warmth and weight of the embrace throughout their own body.

ost with this condition, it seems that the source of the sensation must be visible in order for the empath to experience the tactile effect. This means that a synesthetic empath would need to actually witness someone else being tickled in order to feel as though they were tickled themselves. Unlike the physical empath, if the synesthetic empath encountered an individual who was writhing on the floor in agony, suffering from an internal, invisible pain, such as a severe stomach ache, they most likely would not feel pain in their own gut; they might, however, feel as though their own limbs were being flailed against the ground as they watch the sufferer rolling about, or perhaps feel the tension in their muscles as they wince and squirm.

Synesthetic Empaths as Healers

Empaths who experience synesthesia may have a difficult time working as physical healers, as much of the pain or violence they'll witness will take a serious physical and mental toll on them. However, they are particularly well-suited to bridge the gap between the worlds of medical science and emotional or metaphysical energy, as they are one of the only empath types that are recognized in the scientific realm. They can serve to remind us all of how deeply our actions can impact the people around us, and that pain is a shared experience.

Synesthetic empaths regularly report feeling overwhelmed by human interactions, no matter how mild. As with physical empaths, it is recommended that they offer healing services to one client at a time, in an environment that promotes calm and focus.

Animal Empaths

Animal empaths may carry the same empathic abilities and traits as emotional or physical empaths, but with most of their empathy directed towards animals. Many feel more comfortable in the company of animals than humans and are deeply attuned to the animal's needs, fears, desires, and instincts. Their empathic gifts often endear them to animals, even species that are usually deemed too wild or dangerous to form bonds with humans, and animals tend to be drawn to them in turn, feeling calmer in their presence than they do with other people.

Animal empaths are rarer than emotional or physical empaths, and there is a great deal of diversity amongst them in terms of empathic power. Some are able to sense energies emitted from all non-human animals, while some report connections only with a certain species, or with one specific animal. Some animal empaths simply feel a stronger connection to animals than they do with humans, but still manage to maintain perfectly healthy emotional relationships with other people; by contrast, other animal empaths may struggle to relate to humans generally and find interpersonal relationships extremely challenging.

Most animals are deeply empathic themselves. They need to be, as they do not have the ability to communicate with language but must navigate complex group dynamics to stay safe and well-fed.

The animal empath often views life through the perspective of an animal, rejecting or rebelling against the trappings of modern society, and preferring to focus on the animal necessities of life: food, shelter from danger, comfort, and unity with nature.

Animal Empaths as Healers

Since animal empaths are so sensitive to the energies of animals, they naturally make wonderful veterinarians and caretakers of animals. They can also use their gifts to help humans, though, as animal comfort has proven very effective in treating people with anxiety disorders, depression, and autism, just to name a few conditions. Animals can also be trained to work in service to those with physical or mental disabilities. Animal empaths are uniquely suited to bridge the growing gap between humanity and the animal kingdom, reminding us all to look up to animals instead of looking down on them and to recognize that humans and animals are more similar than we are different.

Plant Empaths

Plant empaths are tapped into the energy of the natural world. They have green thumbs, able to coax plants to grow and thrive, sometimes even under inhospitable conditions, and are more aware than most of the rhythms of nature. Many have no need to consult farmer's almanacs or weather reports to know what's in store for the plants in their garden or farm.

As with animal empaths, the community of plant empaths includes a vast array of different experiences. Some plant empaths get along with other people easily, and simply find that they have a strong penchant for gardening, or feel more comfortable surrounded by a natural landscape; meanwhile, some plant empaths have a very difficult time relating to other humans or animals and tend to use nature as a means of self-isolation. Most plant empaths rely heavily on a physical connection to the natural world in order to feel healthy and happy; in locations where nature is inaccessible, such as deep in the heart of a concrete city, they may quickly become anxious, depressed, or disoriented.

Plant Empaths as Healers

Plant empaths can serve the world as healers in several different fashions. Some plant empaths find their stride in healing other humans and animals through the plant and nutrition-based treatments, working as nutritionists and dieticians, cooks or chefs, homeopathic doctors, crafters of herbal medicine, naturopaths, and so on. Meanwhile, some are better able to apply their healing energies towards plant life exclusively, using their empathic powers to nurture those plants which can best serve the environment, those which can be distilled into medicinal remedies, or those that can best feed their communities.

All plants absorb energy from the sun. Eating an organic, plant-based diet is one of the simplest and most ethically sound ways to consume the energy of life without guilt. Much of the oxygen we breathe is recycled by plants in our environment. The earth's atmosphere and ecosystems rely on thriving plant life to self-sustain. This being the case, many plant empaths are already actively involved in healing efforts without even being aware of it, on a global level. The simple act of nourishing these underserved life forms can have an immeasurable positive impact on society and the environment at large.

Geomantic Empaths

Geomantic empaths feel empathetic connections to natural materials or places rather than with living beings. They may also be referred to as "environmental empaths," and they are able to pick up on the energetic vibrations of rocks, trees, mountains, bodies of water, geographic locations, or even distant celestial bodies. Some also feel an affinity with human-built structures and can recognize the energy of past and future events housed within the walls of certain rooms or buildings.

There are two primary forms of geomantic empathy: object-based, and earth-based. Object-based geomantic empaths will feel connections to specific items or buildings, and typically have a strong preference for positively charged items (those with happy histories) or new items that have an energetic blank slate. For these empaths, vintage shopping can be a challenging, unpredictable experience; even new items that are created or sourced unethically may carry a negative charge that impacts them. Museums and historical landmarks may be emotionally overwhelming. Furthermore, finding a place to live can be quite difficult, as most previously inhabited spaces will retain the energies of previous tenants; even if nothing particularly traumatic occurred in the home, it is likely to feel somewhat haunted until space can be energetically cleansed, through smudging or another cleansing ritual.

Earth-based geomantic empaths, by contrast, feel an empathic connection to the elements of the earth in all their various forms. They resonate with organic materials, no matter how large or small: mountains and pebbles, oceans and raindrops, thriving redwood forests and fallen twigs. Some geomantic empaths claim that they are able to communicate with ancient trees which, like Gods, channel energy, and spiritual wisdom through them.

Occasionally, geomantic empaths are able to sense oncoming natural disasters before they occur. This may sound implausible, but when we look at the animal kingdom, we see that this instinctual detection is not at all uncommon or supernatural in nature; rodents, birds, cats, dogs, horses, and elephants will often panic and attempt to flee in the moments before a natural disaster, like an earthquake or tsunami, strikes. These beings may simply be more sensitive than most to the vibrations of the earth, which do shift subtly during cataclysmic events.

Geomantic Empaths as Healers
Geomantic empaths can be effective healers in several arenas. They can be especially well-suited to energy healing practices that involve crystal work, such as chakra alignment or geomancy.

Geomantic empaths may benefit from the study of the principles of sacred geometry and apply these theories to landscaping or interior design. Empathically informed home and garden design can be an integral aspect of any long-term healing journey.

Rare Empath types

The following categories of empathic power are extremely rare to encounter. This being the case, there are many skeptics who question whether or not these forms of empathic ability actually exist, and judge those who claim to harness them as frauds. Typically, those who are skeptical of these abilities also fail to understand the nuance of these categories, lumping them all together under one umbrella or confusing one type for another. In truth, very few empaths who identify with the below categories claim to possess supernatural abilities, such as telepathy or the ability to move items with the mind. Instead, most simply claim to be able to tap into energetic frequencies that the rest of us are oblivious to.

Furthermore, most will refer to these abilities as "gifts" rather than "powers" because they aren't always able to determine when, where, or how they use them. Often, these empath types receive extra-sensory messages from the universe that are confusing, disjointed, irrelevant to their personal lives, and inconveniently timed. It is very rare for these empaths to find opportunities to use their sensitivities for personal gain, and many have a number of blind spots in their own lives, despite their incredible insight into the lives of others.

Intuitive Empaths (also called Claircognizant Empaths)

The gifts of the Intuitive empath are frequently exaggerated in media depictions, which is perhaps why so many people confuse them with precognitive and channel empaths. Intuitive empaths don't have any more insight into the future than anyone else would, in their position; it's the present that they are especially sensitive to, as they are able to detect more than just the emotional and physical energies of others around them, but also their specific energetic frequencies. This means that while an intuitive empath may not have insight on absolutely everything, like your name, your age, your profession, or where you were born, they might immediately sense upon meeting you that you have butterflies in your stomach because you're falling in love with someone new, or that you are on edge because you narrowly escaped a car accident on your way to see them. An emotional empath would only pick up on another person's feelings, while an intuitive empath is more likely to understand the cause and effect of those emotions.

All of us, even those with very low levels of empathetic sensitivity, take in a great deal of information through our senses (sight, sound, smell, taste, and touch) only for our brains to then sort through and disregard, or block out, the majority of it. Our brains do this automatically, sorting through all perceived information and processing only that which it has been trained to see as important or relevant, in order to protect us from getting overwhelmed. To demonstrate this, lift your eyes from the page, let them gloss over and lose focus, then close them for a few moments. Then open them again, and take note of how quickly your eyes choose to focus on one or two items in your view. Also, take note of just how many details your eyes naturally overlook— the color of the floor, the color of the walls, cracked paint, a pile of dust in the corner, the smear on the window pane. If you couldn't ignore these insignificant details, chances are you'd never be able to form a coherent thought or string a few words together into a sentence, because you'd be drowning in information overload at all times.

Intuitive empaths have to use the same strategy to protect themselves from overstimulation; only they often have to learn to shut out a much larger percentage of the sensory information available to them. Many develop coping mechanisms that numb themselves too much of their empathic sensitivities: alcoholism or substance abuse, sex addiction, gambling, and overeating are fairly common behaviors for this empath type. Claircognizants also have a tendency to self-isolate, as the information they pick up on in social situations can often be jarring, unpleasant, and burdensome to carry.

Furthermore, they should feel encouraged to connect with empathic healers in other categories, as they can often see the bigger picture in any individual's healing journey; for example, when working with an empathic chiropractor, they may be able to help the practitioner to see their client's stress or anxiety as a factor in their discomfort, or note that the root of their pain is actually based on the dysfunction of an internal organ, rather than a skeletal or muscular issue. They also make wonderful matchmakers between healers and patients, able to sense who will work well together, versus those who might struggle to get onto the same page or effectively communicate with one another.

Channel Empaths (also called Mediums)

Empaths who receive messages from deceased spirits and non-human entities are typically called Channels or Mediums. Some are also able to detect energies from other peoples' past lives. Typically, they receive messages from one distinct point beyond the realm of the living and transmit it to one interested party here on earth. Occasionally, this transmission is an all-encompassing experience for the empath, who embodies the spirit's posture, facial expressions, and speech patterns temporarily.

Channel empaths are extremely rare, though there are many who falsely claim to possess these abilities in order for personal gain. A true channel empath would never aim to exploit another person's grief, so they are not likely to solicit clients or push their services upon anyone. The healing that a true channel empath can offer most people is largely emotional, often focused on grief recovery or a return from a crisis in faith.

Precognitive Empaths (also called Psychic Empaths)

A Precognitive empath, commonly called a psychic, is able to pick up on energetic shifts that indicate future events. This type of empath is frequently misunderstood in popular culture, believed to be mostly fraudulent if they are not able to accurately predict every aspect of the future and name all realities of the present. Precognitive empaths do not claim to be omniscient, however; the energies they detect usually provide them with very limited information, most often delivered through cryptic dreams, the unsettling sensation of déjà vu, jarring visions, or symbolic omens. The messages they receive are frequently abstract and difficult to make sense of until elements of the predicted event begin to fall into place.

Precognitive empaths may identify strongly with the myth of Cassandra, who was given the gift of foresight by Apollo, but then cursed by the very same God with the inability to effectively use her knowledge to impact the future. She was cursed so that no one would ever believe her predictions, despite the fact that they were all accurate. Precognitive empaths often struggle with the basics of interpersonal communication and have a hard time making their voices heard. This may be due to the fact that their insight isn't meant to help them to change the future at all, at least not on their own.

Precognitive empaths will often work as fortune-tellers, an arena which allows them to channel their empathic sensitivities while ultimately leaving it up to their clients to decide if their predictions will influence the future or not.

Chapter 3 How to Know If You are an Empath

Recognizing your special gifts as an empath is one of the first steps that you must take in order to properly manage the benefits and challenges of being one. This would also help you create and maintain good relationships with those around you.

The best person to assess whether or not you are an empath is yourself. Even though empathy involves the energy and emotions of other people, this ability is still primarily centered on your personal thoughts and feelings. Hence, the most effective way of confirming this is through a guided self-assessment.

Self-Assessment Test on Empathy

Answer the following questions with either "yes" if condition stated describes you or "no" if you have never felt or thought that way. Keep a tally of your responses so that you can ascertain later on your level of empathy.

Have you ever been labeled as "shy", "introverted," or "highly sensitive"?

Do you often feel worried or overwhelmed?

Do you feel uncomfortable whenever you hear someone yelling, even if it is not aimed at you?

Do arguments make you feel ill, even when you are not involved in it?

Have you ever thought that you do not fit in with the people around you?

Do crowds drain away from your energy?

Have you ever felt the need to isolate yourself from others in order to regain your energy?

Do you get overwhelmed or overstimulated when you hear loud noises?

Do you get overwhelmed or overstimulated when you smell strong odors, regardless of whether the odor is pleasant or not?

Do you get overwhelmed or overstimulated when you are around people who talk incessantly?

Do you get overwhelmed or overstimulated whenever you wear clothes made of itchy fabric?

Do you have the tendency to binge with food and/or drinks in order to cope with stress or pain?

Does your body react strongly to caffeinated drinks?

Does your body react strongly to the side effects of the medication you are taking?

Does the concept of intimate relationships with other people make you feel uneasy?

Does your spouse or intimate partner often make you feel suffocated?

Are you easy to startle?

Do you have a low threshold for pain?

Have you ever observed yourself absorbing the stress felt by those around you?

Have you ever observed yourself absorbing the emotions felt by those around you?

Do you prefer doing your tasks one at a time instead of multitasking?

Do you regenerate your energy by going out for walks or hikes?

Do you need a long time to regain your energy after spending time with energy vampires?

Do you prefer living in a small town rather than in big cities?

Do you prefer engaging with a few people only rather than joining a large gathering of people?

Once you have answered each question, get the total number of "yes" responses you have given. Decode the meaning by matching your total with the following:

1 to 7 "yes" responses: You have a low level of empathy.

8 to 12 "yes" responses: You are exhibiting signs of moderate empathic abilities.

13 to 17 "yes" responses: You have a high level of empathy.

17 to 25 "yes" responses: You are a full-fledged empath.

Getting a confirmation that you are an empath is an important step in taking control over your special abilities. Instead of simply wondering whether your experiences are signs of being an empath, you have taken a proactive approach by going through the guide questions given above. From here on, you would be able to form better means of self-care and improve your relationships with those you care about.

The Differences between Sensitive People and Empaths

Some literature on empathy use the terms "sensitive person" and "empath" interchangeably. This is inaccurate for there are key differences between these two types of people. The confusion is understandable, however. According to experts, all empaths are sensitive, but not all sensitive people possess the gift of empathy.

To further elaborate the differences, here are the key distinctions that separate one from the other:

Sensitivity

Sensitive people are highly aware of their surroundings, even of the subtle changes that average individuals overlook. Because of this, they can easily be overwhelmed by the large amounts of stimuli that are beyond their control.

These traits are also present among empaths. However, their level of sensitivity goes beyond their physical senses. Empaths pick up the emotions and energies of the people around them and then take them on as if they were their own. They literally experience whatever the other person is feeling. As such, they can get overwhelmed not just by their surroundings, but also by the strong emotions felt by people nearby.

Processing of Highly Emotional Situations

Sensitive people can get affected by the extremely positive and negative emotions of others. For example, they feel miserable when a friend suffers from a tragedy. They do not, however, feel the same level of pain and despair as the other person does. What they are feeling is their own pain from seeing others in such a state. The emotions are their own, though it has been triggered by an external factor.

Empaths, on the other hand, would go through the experience as they are personally going through the same tragedy. Aside from misery and pain, they would also absorb the anxiety, physical pain, and stress levels of the other person. If they would or could not remove themselves from that situation, the empath would exhibit the same emotions and pains as the other person does. For example, if the person gets a migraine from crying, the empath would also develop a migraine just because they are nearby that grieving person.

Ability to Read the Emotions of Other People

Because they are feeling their own emotions, sensitive people tend to view others through the lens of how they are feeling now. They do not completely understand where the other person is coming from, or why the person is feeling happy, sad, or upset. Instead, they project their personal issues on others and assume what others might be feeling based on they would react if they were in that situation.

In comparison, empaths are inherently sensitive towards non-verbal cues that give away the true emotions of other people. Over time and with regular practice, they can be effective at reading between the lines, especially when one's words do not match the emotions that are being picked up by the empath. Instead of projecting outwards, empath draws in the emotions of others and process them accordingly.

To clarify, empaths and sensitive people differ primarily on their capability to pick up and understand the emotions of others. Though every empath is also considered as sensitive, not all sensitive people are empaths as well. Therefore, before you label yourself as an empath, check first if you possess the general qualities observed among empaths.

Chapter 4 Empaths, emotions, and health: How to stop absorbing other people's distress

The concept of empathy is often described as something interchangeable with sympathy, but in reality, the two words describe vastly different internal thought processes. Sympathy is a theoretical emotive response and one which is generally chosen rather than experienced involuntarily. Usually, even if we aren't conscious of the thought process, we decide whether or not others are deserving of our sympathy before we allow ourselves to be emotionally moved. This is perhaps why so many of the homeless who sustain themselves on spare change feel the need to hold signs that explain how they came to find themselves in such a position, or remind others of their own humanity and victimization; without these props to elicit sympathy, many passers-by would presume this person to be a criminal or a hopeless addict, and excuse themselves from the act of sympathizing, choosing to ignore or even antagonize them based on a split-second judgment.

When we see or hear about another person's suffering, we often express our sympathy by saying something along the lines of: "I feel bad for this individual." Usually, what we mean by this is actually closer to the following sentiment: "I understand this individual's suffering on a theoretical level, and I would feel very badly if I were standing in their shoes."

Empathy, by contrast, removes the hypothetical aspect of this thought process, closing the cognitive distance between the sufferer and the compassionate observer. For many people, empathy also removes the aspect of choice. When we empathize with someone else, we don't just imagine that we would feel bad if we were in their position; instead of feeling bad for another person, we feel badly right along with them, and the emotional responses they stir up within us are often overwhelming, involuntary, and difficult to shake. We experience another person's pain, sorrow, anger, excitement, fear, humiliation, joy, or confusion, as though it were our own emotional burden to carry.

Whereas many people infer a connotation to negative emotions when they think of sympathy, empathy can allow us to experience the full range of emotional, and sometimes physical, responses, whether positive, negative, or somewhere in between, as we detect these sensations in others. Think of a wedding guest who is moved to tears of joy while watching the ceremony; this person most likely isn't crying because they feel sad, nor because they feel a sense of sympathy for the couple, but rather because they are able to empathize with the couple and other members of the wedding party, overwhelmed by all of the powerful emotional energies flowing through the room. This type of empathetic response can also apply to emotional sensations that are more confusing or difficult to name; for instance, a highly empathetic person might feel an unsettling mix of unrecognizable emotions in an environment full of cognitive dissonance, or when surrounded by liars. As compared to sympathy, empathy is a far more immediate, compulsive, and multidimensional experience. There is usually a limit to how much sympathy we can feel or express for another person; however, with empathy, the potential for depth and breadth of emotional connection is boundless.

The Science of Empathy

Empaths and empath healers are more widely recognized and appreciated outside the realms of western medicine and science. Some skeptics balk at the term "empath" and question the existence of such an identity, believing it to be synonymous with the supernatural and metaphysical only, rather than something rooted in reality. Some are unwilling to believe anything they cannot see proven in scientifically measurable terms.

These naysayers might be surprised to learn that there is a great deal of scientific evidence to support not only the existence of measurable empathetic responses in most humans, but also the existence of hyper-empathetic individuals, or empaths.

There is no question that empathy itself is as real as rock, both demonstrable and measurable. Each of us is gifted with a mirror-neuron system (though it is more active in some than others) that allows us to connect to the observed experiences of others. This is most likely an evolutionary tool to promote self-preservation, as it causes us to be more alert and attentive when we see another person in danger or pain and take steps to avoid repeating their fate. The mirror-neuron system also helps us to feel happy when we see others having fun or to feel hungry when we see others eating a hearty meal. It is also why sad movies can move us to tears and why pornography has the power to excite us sexually. Mirror-neurons often inspires involuntary and subconscious reactions; we yawn when we see someone else yawning, and automatically smile or scowl to reflect the facial expression of anyone addressing us. We even feel the impulse to mimic foreign accents after just a few minutes of conversation with someone whose speech pattern differs from our own.

It is a scientific fact—not metaphysical theory—that our physical actions impact our emotions and thoughts. A sad person who holds a pencil in between their teeth can quickly trick their own brain into believing that they have something to smile about; if a smile is inspired, instead, by the sight of someone else smiling, the emotional impact is the same. Our mirror-neurons can literally make emotions contagious, pushing us to feel the same way as the people around us do.

Furthermore, it has been scientifically proven that a small percentage of the population possesses overactive mirror-neuron systems. These people mimic even the subtlest of behavioral shifts, and their impulse to mirror observed behavior is both immediate and overpowering. While the term "empath" may not garner much respect or acceptance in the world of science, evidence to support the existence of empaths is irrefutable.

The Evolutionary Purpose of Empathy

Empathy is easily observable in most infants and young children. Infants in neonatal wards will most often exhibit contagious crying; one baby will begin to wail over genuine discomfort, but the surrounding children will most often join in soon thereafter, unable to distinguish between their own emotions and the pain of others. As they grow into toddlerhood, most children will continue to exhibit involuntary empathy, mirroring the facial expressions of the adults in their lives, even without understanding the motivations behind these emotions. Children need to be hyper-empathetic during these developmental stages; this is how they learn to interact with other humans, even before they are able to speak.

Most often, as children continue to grow and begin to grasp the language as a communicative tool, they will still experience contagious crying, infectious laughter, and other emotional states as though they are viral. However, during these developmental years, children raised in healthy and supportive environments will also begin to learn to differentiate their own emotions, physical feelings, and needs from those that rightfully belong to other people. This is the stage at which most children learn to advocate for themselves. Depending on how their empathetic or self-serving behaviors are received, they will eventually settle into a style of empathetic connection (or lack thereof) that allows them to feel safe and accepted. A child raised in a chaotic or volatile environment may detach from their empathic impulses in order to protect themselves; meanwhile, an only child of an emotionally repressed parent may develop hyper-empathy so that they can still feel their parent's love, even when it isn't expressed.

It seems that almost every position on the empathy scale, no matter how healthy or destructive it may appear, is valuable to the function of society at large—even those who are so deficient in empathy as to become violent. Those who are highly empathic tend to be community-minded, focused on what serves and protects everyone; those who are empathy-deficient, by contrast, are more likely to focus on the single-minded pursuit of their personal goals. Together, these types create a balance between thought and action, practicality and emotionality, forward momentum and retrospection. The empath tends to be more open-minded, tolerant, and giving, while those who are empathy-deficient are often defensive, judgmental, and focused on self-preservation above all else. When it comes to managing resources and establishing cultural values, there is a place for both points of view within any community.

Empathy vs. Empathic Sensitivity

Many people suffer from the misconception that empaths are defined simply as people who are capable of feeling and expressing empathy; in truth, though, everyone is capable of accessing empathy, even malignant narcissists. The trick is to evaluate whether or not that empathy is voluntary. A malignant narcissist may sometimes choose to exercise their empathetic muscle as a means to manipulate others, or to endear themselves to a strategic target. A person who falls in the "normal" empathetic range will most likely feel involuntarily compelled to empathize with those they love or those who remind them of themselves. Meanwhile, a true empath is often unable to discriminate in this arena; they compulsively empathize with loved ones and strangers alike, with both victims and aggressors, even sometimes with people who have caused the empath direct and purposeful harm.

Most people automatically work to distance themselves from empathetic connections that are unpleasant or seem potentially dangerous. Empaths, meanwhile, are usually only able to do this through extensive training. Furthermore, people who fall into the normal range of empathy learn to notice that which is relevant to their experience and ignore that which is not—they can pass a crying stranger on the street without giving them a second thought, but when their best friend is in tears, they become hyper-alert and observative. Those who are empathy-deficient generally only take note of things that impact them directly, so they aren't likely to care much about anyone's tears except their own. By contrast, a true empath will often give equal emotional and mental weight to everything they take note of; to them, there is no difference between the tears of a stranger on the street, tears falling from their best friend's eyes, tears that fall on the opposite side of the planet, and tears that stream down their own cheeks.

Common Traits of an Empath

The empath community is home to a cast of unique characters; that being said, there are a number of common traits that empaths of all types tend to exhibit. Here is a list of just a few of those traits. There are many, many more, which I invite you to discover by reaching out to other empaths and sharing your experiences.

Empaths tend to be...

Extremely sensitive, both emotionally and physically

Introverted, or easily overwhelmed by a lack of privacy or alone time

Creative minded and expressive

Overly generous

Diplomatic

Detail-oriented

Sometimes absent-minded or forgetful

Peacemakers

Picky about the things they consume (from food to television, to the energy source that fuels their home or car)

Chronically fatigued

People pleasers

Free spirits and wanderers

Frequently suffering from lower back pain and indigestion.

Nature lovers and animal enthusiasts

Surrounded by people who rely on their support, advice, guidance, and compassion.

Quiet and reserved

Deep thinkers

The Empath and the Highly Sensitive Person

While the empathic identity may still be viewed as a fringe concept by some in the fields of psychology and social work, Highly Sensitive People, or HSPs, are commonly recognized within both fields. Some literature may refer to empaths and HSPs interchangeably, equating the two identities; while they have a great deal in common, there are some noted differences between a Highly Sensitive Person and an empath. The chances are that most empaths are also HSPs (but not all); conversely, there are likely many Highly Sensitive People who are not especially empathetic or empathic.

The primary difference seems to lie in the way each identity processes their emotional responses to information. Both HSPs and empaths are more likely than others to notice minor details and small behavioral shifts in other people; both have a tendency to feel emotions more deeply than others and to pick up on energies that aren't their own.

Yet the Highly Sensitive Person generally seems able to differentiate between the emotions and physical sensations that should rightfully be their own, and those of others; in fact, some report that emotional contagion from others often feels physically invasive or threatening, and inspires a visceral reaction that prompts them to strictly enforce their boundaries and distance themselves from any energy source that feels overwhelming. Some HSPs can actually grow quite detached from their empathetic impulses, using impassivity as a shield and emotional isolation as a survival mechanism. Their heightened sensitivity does not necessarily inspire them to share in the emotions they detect in others; they may present as more judgmental than compassionate and understanding (though this is not always the case).

Empaths, by contrast, will always struggle to remain unaffected by external energies unless they take specific precautions to keep themselves balanced, guarded, and consistently replenished. They often feel that their connections to others are obligatory and that they do not have a choice in the matter.

Though different studies and sources tend to report varied numbers, it is generally believed that only about one or two percent of the population could be diagnosed as hyper-empathetic or empathic. Meanwhile, it is estimated that as much as twenty percent of the population might identify as highly sensitive. It is possible that HSPs are repressed or disempowered empaths, and that most could be trained to enhance their sensitivities to the level of empathic power with the right guidance and support from experienced empaths.

Chapter 5 Empaths, love, and sex

Empaths spend their lives going out of their way for all sorts of people, including complete strangers. They share their emotions and respond to their needs. They share their emotions and respond to their needs. How much deeper is the connection if they actually fall in love? Empaths love deeply, which is beautiful, in this era of superficial relationships. If they find the right person, then they are in for a blissful, romantic relationship.

Empaths love in peculiar ways. If you are lucky enough to be loved by an empath, your union will be:

·   Intense: when empaths love, they love for real. The love is pure, selfless and deep. In addition, they can feel your emotions even before you communicate them, and respond appropriately.

·   Honest: empaths don't tolerate lies. They tell the truth as it is; without manipulations or mind games. You'll always know where your relationship stands. Don't lie to them either; remember they can 'read your thoughts'.

·   Loyal: empaths are highly sensitive to any form of negativity, and will be the last people to cause it. They will always do what is right for the relationship. They know what it is like to be broken, and would never want to subject you to that. You're in safe hands!

·   Selfless: they freely share their time, energy and resources with you. Since loving and caring comes naturally to them, you'll enjoy being the center of their attention. Even when they're feeling overwhelmed, which is pretty often, they will still attend to you. They not only want you to be happy, but they also need you to be happy. Remember they absorb emotions, so when you're experiencing joy, so are they.

· Considerate: highly sensitive people are often in pain due to the myriad of emotions bombarding them. Yet they'll not expose the pain to you. They will find a way of dealing with their emotions without burdening you.

· Long-term: the relationship will be based on a deep connection. Empaths don't do flings. They dive right into the deep end. They don't fall in love easily, but once you're in their heart, you're in. They will easily overlook your mistakes, and forgive time and again. They will give the relationship another chance even when others would have walked out.

Being loved by an empath is truly blissful. Unlike others who may demand your attention every other time, empaths do not mind spending time by themselves every so often. If anything, they need that time to recharge from their physical and emotional fatigue. They are not clingy, so you will have no problem retaining your space.

Sex also happens differently for an empath. Since empaths are highly sensitive to energy, sex cannot be casual. During sex, energies combine, and they pick up the emotions of the partner. If the partner is happy and positive, then the lovemaking is absolute bliss. On the other hand, if the partner is experiencing sadness, anger or fear, the negative energy is shared as well, ruining the experience for an empath. A sexual empath is somebody whose empathic capacity intensifies during sex.

Falling in love with a fellow empath

Can you imagine a romantic relationship with a partner who is equally highly sensitive? It's euphoric at best. It is estimated that empaths form 15-20% of the population. This means that there is still a fair chance that you meet your fellow empath and fall in love.

A relationship of empaths is a pure delight in many ways. Are you going through life feeling like nobody understands you? Have you been feeling others yet they don't feel you? With a fellow empath, you eventually get someone who can return the favor. The connection will be soul deep. Your communication begins even before you utter a single word. You can feel each other's thoughts and emotions.

Two empaths make two givers. Here you will not only be giving but receiving as well. You both nurture and take care of each other. You tend to each other's deepest needs since you can feel them even when they are not communicated aloud. The surprises will be awesome. You'll receive what you need and when you need it. If you're sad, your partner can feel it and surprise you with something cheerful. If you're anxious, your partner will step in to reassure you. The love and care will flow between the two of you.

The sex is magical as well. Since your energies connect, you will be in perfect sync, the kind where you do not know where one stopped and the other began. You will feel each other's needs, so you know exactly how to respond. Yours will be a merging of bodies, souls and spirits; just an incredible experience.

Your common love for animals will give you an amazing connection with your pets. Empathy allows you to feel the emotions of animals as well. Your furry friends will have the time of their lives in your household. On a larger scale, you can start an animal shelter and share love and compassion with needy animals.

You both value alone time, so you will easily allow it. A non-empath may not understand why you keep spending time away from him/her. That may very well be a major bond of contention. 'Are you ignoring me? Is there a problem with our relationship? Are we breaking up?' Such are the questions you may have to contend with every time you take time out for yourself. With a fellow empath, you can take time as often and as for long as you like.

Any downside to a relationship of empaths? Well, quite a number. Your deep connection is for the most part, but can routinely work against you. Imagine a situation where your partner is sad or angry, yet does not show it outwardly. You begin to feel similar emotions, and you are wondering what is happening since your lover seems happy. Confusing; isn't it? Similarly, imagine that one of you is happy and the other is sad. And there you are absorbing each other's emotions. Your moods will fluctuate up and down, which is destabilizing.

You will know things about each other before they are even mentioned since you already feel them. This is not always a good thing. Ideally, people should choose what they want to share and what they want to keep to themselves for personal reasons. They can also be willing to share, just not yet. With empaths, this is hardly possible. As soon as you feel it, it is out there. You do not get the time to process your feelings and determine the suitable course of action. This way, you find yourselves in each other's business all the time, and this can cause friction.

Ultimately, the pros far outweigh the cons of empath relationships. If you get the opportunity to be loved by someone who is just like you, by all means, take it. You will share a deep, beautiful bond that many others can only dream of.

Common mistakes empaths make in relationships

This refers to a case where you are the empath but your partner is not. Your partner may be experiencing a blissful relationship, but you are not. Unfortunately, many empaths, even with all their goodness, often experience toxic relationships. Your partner could be taking advantage of your empathic abilities. Here are pitfalls that you are likely to fall into:

a) Give too much

You feel that you cannot or should not say no. You give too much of your time, energy and resources. You mirror a child/parent relationship, where you're the one making most of the effort. Remember as a healer, you're most likely to attract the wounded. So here, you are with a partner with plenty of baggage, and you feel the need to attend to their every need.

Unfortunately, there are those who will come to your life with selfish intentions. They spot a giver, and they want to be constant takers. They do not really care about you. In addition to sharing your empathy with the world, they also demand your constant attention. If you have some savings or a well-paying job, they can easily con you. You have to learn to set boundaries here. You cannot be everything for anyone. Even if they have had rough patches in the past, you should not be the one to heal them. Giving too much will leave you drained, and still not guarantee you a steady relationship.

b) Forgive unconditionally

You insist on seeing the best in people, even when they show you who they really are. You make excuses for their behavior. They may cheat and lie time and again, yet you'll still forgive. Forgiveness has its place in relationships, but it should have conditions. You should at least have a promise that the mistake will not be repeated. Your partner could be intentionally misbehaving, knowing that your empathic nature will lead you to forgive yet again.

So here, you are going out of your way to do what you think is right for your relationship, but you only end up being hurt.

c) Stay too long

Even when a relationship is not working, you will continue to stay and attempt to fix it. You do most of the work; giving, caring, nurturing and anything else that it will take to revive the relationship. If your partner is not reciprocating, you'll wear yourself out. You feel the relationship is not good for you, but your fear hurting your companion by admitting so, much less leaving.

People stay in relationships because of love, you stay because of guilt. You are the sacrificial lamb. You end up sad, angry and feeling wasted. And you miss the opportunity to be with someone who is truly good for you.

Leaving a wrong relationship does not make you any less empathic. Look at it like this: you are also giving the person an opportunity to get into an authentic, loving relationship with someone else. It is a win both ways; isn't it?

d) Prioritize your partner

Your own needs come first in a relationship. An empath will need to read that again. You're the vessel that gives, nurtures and cares for others. If that vessel is worn out, then nobody is getting any service. You should first make sure that you're healthy and whole.

Remember your partner is not there to complete you, but to complement you. You should be bringing your best self to the table. Take time to cater to your physical, emotional and spiritual needs. You are your own responsibility, just as your partner is. You only give the best when you are at your best. And that will only be achieved if you put you first.

Empaths largely have challenges in matters of love when they fall in the hands of inconsiderate people. Since they give so readily, they attract many people whose need is just receiving. Others attract even worse; sociopaths or psychopaths who do not care about anybody else but themselves. The empaths work themselves silly trying to take care of and please their partners. They receive little in return. They end up distressed and exhausted. And even then, they have a hard time leaving.

Ideally, empaths ought to be treasured and appreciated for their gift. They're the minority anyway, so anyone who gets the opportunity to be in a relationship with an empath is extremely lucky. Just as they give; they should receive too. Remember they spend the whole day catering to people around them and feeling their emotions. By the time they come home; they're worn out. Their partners need to take time to pamper them, so they can rejuvenate.

As an empath, use your intuitive ability to gauge those around you. Are they attracted to you as a person or are they just after what you give? Beware of people with no good intentions. Should you be fortunate enough to meet and fall in love with a fellow empath, you're lucky. If not, look out for someone who takes time to understand your personality, and is willing to reciprocate what you do for him/her. For the deep love that you give, you should be loved back just as intensely.

Sabotaging Your Relationships

The way you relate to others and yourself tends to change because of your empathic abilities. In a manner of speaking, your heart is open to other people's emotions and emotional baggage. This can become too much to handle. A lot of people wrongly assume that it is easier for an empath to navigate the troubles of relationships. However, the opposite is true. The mind and heart of an empath functions at a higher frequency and might not necessarily be at the same level as that of their partner. So, it is quite common for an empath's relationship to follow atypical patterns. This certainly comes with its own set of pros and cons.

In this section, you will learn about the ways you might be sabotaging your relationship as an empath. By recognizing these signs, you can take corrective action immediately. This, in turn, will make it easier to navigate any relationship in your life.

Compromising the boundaries

Empaths tend to compromise on their boundaries even when the partner hasn't asked them to. Usually, it is an empath's inherent tendency to place the needs of their partner above their own. Because of their overpowering desire to help others, they end up compromising their personal boundaries. When an empath starts doing this, especially when their partner hasn't asked them to, it can build up resentment and even anger toward the other person. Since their partner is not even aware of the sacrifice made by the empath, it is quite unlikely that their partner will acknowledge the same. This can just make empaths feel exhausted, tired, and frustrated with the relationship. If you are used to doing this in your relationships, then keep in mind that you are essentially sabotaging a healthy relationship. Instead of swooping in to help, ask your partner if he needs any help. Keep the channels of communication open. Don't assume, discuss.

Why go through this trouble when your partner isn't even aware of it? Don't give a chance for resentment to build up. It will slowly eat away at a healthy relationship.

Express your needs

This step is closely associated with the previous step. Keep in mind that your needs are as important and valid as those of your partner. So, don't hesitate to express your needs. Just because you're in a relationship doesn't mean that you don't need to focus on yourself. Don't become so involved with making your partner's needs your only priority that you start neglecting your own. As an empath, it is quite likely that you forget the importance of expressing your needs and wants. A relationship is a two-way street. You can't keep concentrating on one person all the time. If you do this, you will end up feeling neglected or unloved. If you don't express yourself, how will your partner never understand you? So, don't suppress your needs and express yourself.

Self-care

You will obviously feel a deep concern for others. If you are not careful, then this kind of thinking will cost you your emotional well-being. If you start focusing too much on your partner, you might start neglecting the things that make you who you are as a person. It might mean that you spend more time doing things that make your partner happy and stop doing things that make you happy. Don't stop spending time with your loved ones or focusing on your hobbies or anything else that you feel is meaningful merely because your partner has different interests. If you keep doing this, over time, your happiness, and self-esteem, will take a beating. All of this will sabotage your relationship. Also, if you change yourself too much, your partner will start questioning the relationship as well. You don't have to change yourself for others to love you. Start loving yourself for who you are, and your partner will do too. If your partner cannot see this, then maybe does something wrong with the relationship itself.

Not sharing

A relationship cannot function like it's supposed to if the concept of sharing doesn't exist. You must not only share your happiness with each other but your sorrows as well. When you share your troubles with your partner, it means you are letting them in. If you don't share your worries, how will your partner ever know what plagues your mind and heart? You don't have to solve everything on your own, and you can count on your partner. If you feel like you cannot, then maybe it is time to rethink your relationship.

A parent-child relationship

Every empath has an inherent inclination to nurture others. Their desire to do this can often put them in a fiduciary place of power. You might be compelled to help your partner and meet their needs even before they start expressing it. You certainly have their best intentions in mind, but over time, it will seem overbearing to your partner. For a relationship to work, both the partners must treat each other as equals. If you assume the role of a fiduciary authority, you are essentially transforming even a romantic relationship into a parent-child relationship. Give your partner their space, allow them to ask you for help, and don't try to be a parent. You can help them without encroaching into their personal space.

Most of the problems in a relationship can be resolved by opening up channels of communication. Communicate openly, honestly, and freely with each other. If you do this, you can maintain a healthy relationship.

Balance Being An Empath

It is not easy to go through life when you keep absorbing other people's emotions. It can often make you feel pressured and even exhausted. Many people will not understand your struggles of being an empath. Not a lot of people have to experience all the things that you do, so it is not likely that they can understand you. This makes it quite difficult for your relationship to work. Empaths are extremely sensitive to emotional energy. So, they tend to feel stressed or drained out even when they are actively doing anything. Any unstable emotions that they feel can prompt them to make bad decisions. This is perhaps one of the main reasons why empaths struggle in relationships. The close of an empath relationship one has with someone else, the more sensitive they become to their emotions. All this sensitivity can become rather overwhelming for an empath, and it can become too much to handle.

Well, it is safe to say that being an empath can be a blessing and a curse. At times you might feel like there is no escaping what you feel, and you will want to shut yourself out from everything. However, this does not mean that your ability to choose has been taken away from you. You certainly tend to soak up the energy of others, but what makes you truly special is your ability to be loving, kind, and compassionate toward everyone. Since you are blessed with the ability to understand others, it is time to make the most of this.

A common struggle a lot of empaths face is that a relationship can become quite stressful or strenuous for them. Since they feel so deeply for the people they're involved with, they struggle to differentiate their own emotions from others. This can be slightly problematic because the person they love is also the source of the pain. So, empaths must always learn to distinguish their emotions from others and use their empathic ability to make their relationships work. In this section, you will learn about a couple of simple tips you can use to balance being an empath in relationships.

It is not right or wrong to feel any negative emotions. Emotions help us grow the exact same way as any experience would. Whenever you see your loved one in pain, keep in mind that it is a part of life and that there is a lesson to be learned. There might not always be something that you can fix. At times, the best thing you can do is to allow things to be the way they are and trust your partner to fix it. You don't always have to swoop in and help them.

Assessing your emotions

If you cannot assess your emotions, it will prove to be a major hurdle in any relationship. You don't always have to understand what you're feeling. At times, an emotion might not send make sense immediately, but eventually, it will. So, stop being too hard on yourself. Don't be under any misconception that being happy and doing the right thing means the same. At times, you might do something that you don't want to, but it might be the right thing to do.

Being okay

It is time that you understand that you can be okay even when others are not. This is not something you have to feel guilty about.

A common problem of being an empath is that you tend to feel like you cannot be okay unless everyone around you is fine. This isn't possible, and you can't ensure it. Life is unpredictable, and you can't expect everyone to be okay all the time. If you believe that you cannot be okay if others are not, then it will merely cause unnecessary stress. So, why are you putting all this unnecessary stress on yourself? It is time to let go of this. You are not responsible for what others feel, so stop believing otherwise. Whatever others experience is on them, and it might even be necessary for their growth.

Don't keep saying yes

Empaths hate confrontations and are people pleasers. They like to make others happy, and this means they often agree to things even when they don't want to. At times, in your best interest, it is a good idea to say no. Don't say yes because you think it will make someone else happy. Whatever you do must never come at great personal cost. If something feels wrong, then don't go ahead with it. Learn to understand that in a healthy relationship, your partner will accept and respect your 'no.' You don't have to say yes to make others happy. Also, by saying 'no,' you can prevent any codependency from creeping into the relationship. Don't think that it makes you a selfish person if you say 'no,' and don't allow anyone else to tell you otherwise. It also helps set personal boundaries and promote growth within your relationship. When your partner understands and respects all the things you are comfortable with and uncomfortable with, it becomes easier to be with each other.

Time to unplug

Every empath needs some time to unwind and recharge themselves. If you feel like everything is becoming claustrophobic for you and that you aren't able to breathe properly, it is high time that you take a break. Take some time out and unplug yourself from the world. This will help regain your composure and reflect on what might have caused such a reaction. By becoming aware of these triggers, you can prevent the repetition of such events in the future. Try to accept yourself as you are. Don't stop yourself from feeling your true emotions. Learn to accept yourself and your boundaries. Only when you do this will others respect you for the same.

Stop seeking validation

Your emotions and feelings are valid. You don't need the validation of others for them to be true. What you feel matters so stop ignoring it. Don't try to suppress your emotions. If you do this, then sooner or later you will end up having an emotional outburst. At times, you might feel quite disturbed. However, the beauty of life is that things change, and nothing stays the same. So, if you're going through anything, keep in mind that it too shall pass like everything else. Also, stop seeking validation from others. It is time to understand that others must value you for who you are and not for who they think you are.

Being an empath is your strength, and it does not make you weak. Finding the right balance will strengthen your relationship and make you happy. Keep in mind that there is nothing wrong with you, and it is okay to be an empath. Just like the Bruno Mars song, "You are perfect just the way you are." Learn to love yourself first and only then will others love you.

Chapter 6 Empaths and Work

As an empath, you will face particular challenges in the workplace. Everyone deserves a job that fits their abilities and personality, but you need to take extra care before accepting a position because a toxic work environment can make you emotionally, spiritually, and physically sick – fast. So, as an empath, how can you pick the right kind of job and thrive at work?

Now, let's talk about the workplace. Sure, some empaths do have it easier than others are able to choose a suitable job for the empathic person. For the most part, the basic needs are simple it just has to be fulfilling and stress-free.

A job that maximizes their gifts is great too, something that many empaths would often go after. A job that provides them with an outlet for their quiet nature, creativity and intuition is highly recommended.

Some of the best careers for empaths would be those where they need to deal with only a few people. Most of them would be happiest in smaller companies or working from home where they have more control over who they interact with. Office intrigue isn't something that an empath would enjoy nor partake in.

Freelancing is also another option as it enables them to meet new people, but still have control over it. Flexibility in a job is a very important consideration, especially when it comes to time as they would need regular breaks in order to recover lost energy.

Many would choose self-employment for this reason, as it enables them to avoid the pressure of needing to deal with office hierarchy. If they can work within their own time, even better! Rigid schedules are not their thing and they perform better if they can work at their own pace.

There are empaths that do thrive in an office environment as well. However, this depends on a number of different conditions. For example, if the people surrounding them are all relatively positive this energy motivates an empath.

Which jobs are empaths drawn to? Well, whenever they opt to be self-employed, you'll find that empaths do excellent as editors, writers, artists, medical professionals, and any job in the creative field.

Other career options include: graphic and website design, accountants, lawyers with private practices, virtual assistants, independent plumbers and electricians all of whom are capable of setting up their own schedule.

There would be those who can even do well in business consulting and real estate; however, they need to be able to work at their own pace as well. Those with a keenness for nature would do well as forest rangers, landscape designers, as well as horticulturists.

As mentioned earlier, there are also those who prefer taking on professions wherein they can help other people. Many empaths often choose to become social workers, teachers, nurses, therapists anything that brings them closer to others in order to provide some degree of healing.

Some do well in animal rescue and non-profit organizations; all of which are very fulfilling jobs, something that an empath is drawn to. Of course, these are also careers that can be highly stressful, and as such, an empath would need to learn how to protect them from being consumed by work. Regular breaks would be necessary so they can refuel.

It is necessary for empaths to feel stimulated by the job they have chosen. Their skills should be put to use and their talents, maximized. Sure, they may not be the type to thrive in big corporations, professional sports, academia, the military, and government duties, but they can still contribute greatly to whichever career they decide to take on.

The thing with empaths is that they know themselves very well they know what they can do and how that can help. They are full of energy if they love what they're doing, if it is a job they're completely passionate about. For these people, money is just cherry on top of the cake. Their personal needs must be met first. Impractical, yes, but this is simply how these people function. Passion above all else!

Alright, now that we have possible careers outlined, let's talk about what are some of the jobs that an empath should avoid? Now, this doesn't mean that they would be incapable in these jobs. Rather, it only points to the high level of stress and energy demand that these jobs entails things that may not be healthy for an empath and may cause them to feel exhausted quickly. Many of these jobs also undermine their empathic nature.

One such profession would be sales. Given that this is a very extroverted job in nature, empaths might find it difficult to keep up. This is especially so if they encounter aggressive clients. Keep in mind that empaths, such as yourself, do absorb the energy from the environment you're in. If you encounter a number of rowdy people all day long, you will end up drained and burnt out.

The same applies to jobs in politics, public relations, as well as executive work where dealing with large groups of people is a constant. These are jobs that don't really require introspection or sensitivity instead, it's all talk and talk. Aggressively pushing products and ideas forward are things that empaths don't do too well at.

Corporate work is a big no-no for them. The mentality within the environment of big corporations can be extremely exhausting for empaths. These are places that do not give much value to an individual's needs and output is of great importance.

There is a rigid structure that must be followed; schedules, deadlines these are things that many empaths seek to avoid. Their lifestyle and way of thing wouldn't fit in well with it.

That said, there are certain times when an empath might not be able to avoid being in a job that they don't necessarily like.

Everyone has to live and money is a factor in that, right? So, what can they do to improve their situation whilst taking advantage of their inherent skill? It's learning how to adapt to the environment. Learning how to read people can be important as well in order to avoid unnecessary confrontations.

To help with that, here are three simple techniques that you can try:

Observing Body Language Cues.

Research shows that words can only account for about 7% of how we communicate. Body language, on the other hand, accounts for about 55%, whilst voice tone comes in at 30%. Now, how is this useful? For empaths, this would be useful in determining if the person they're speaking to is genuinely interested in their conversation.

They can take certain movements as cues as to where they should nudge the topic towards. That said, this can lead to them becoming too analytical as well so find a balance. Instead of focusing too much on how the person is reacting, just stay fluid and relax.

Be comfortable and stay true to yourself. Do not try too hard to get the person to show interest nor should you feel bad if it happens that they are not always reacting positively.

Pay Attention to Appearance

Ask yourself, what is the first thing you notice when you meet other people for the first time? It is likely that you first pay attention to what they're wearing before moving on to any other feature. Are they dressed properly? Do they look shabby?

We tend to gather our first impression of someone based upon how they look. If a person is well-dressed, we immediately associate that with a healthy well being. On the other hand, if a person looks shabby then we tend to see them as unhealthy or someone who is untrustworthy.

Notice Posture

Another thing we unconsciously pay attention to is a person's posture. How confident do they look? Do they look shy or are they cowering as you speak to them? These are also keys to their personality as well as how comfortable they feel around you. Next time you speak with someone, observe where their hands are. If it's folded across their chest, this is a sign of defensiveness or wariness.

On the other hand, if their arms are comfortably placed somewhere around their body, in their pockets for example, then this means they're quite comfortable with speaking to you. People who are like this tend to be more open conversationalists as well.

Watch For Physical Movements

Observe the way people lean and the distance at which they do. The idea here is that people lean forward or towards people we like whilst we lean away from people we are not too fond of.

As mentioned earlier, crossed arms and legs are both signs of defensiveness. In some cases, they could also point to anger or self-protection. Another thing to look for is where people point their toes at most individuals would point their toes towards the person they feel most comfortable with.

Pay attention to people's hands

When people have their hands on their laps, in their pockets or behind their back, this suggests that they might be hiding something. Whilst this isn't always an accurate observation, it is stills something that you should try and pay more attention to.

Lip biting

Whenever people do this, it is their way of soothing themselves under pressure or after a rather awkward encounter/situation. The same applies to cuticle picking observe children who have a habit of doing this. They tend to be some of the shyest ones.

Interpreting Facial Expressions

Emotions can sometimes be easily read upon people's faces. Frowning suggests worry or overthinking. Pursed lips might mean contempt, anger, or bitterness. Crow's feet could point to the fact that this person is quite jolly, often smiling and simply easygoing. A clenched jaw, however, can signal tension.

Listen to Your Intuition.

It might take some practice, but you can develop the skill of being able to tune into someone's energy beyond simply reading their language and words. This is where your intuitiveness will come in handy. Intuition is what your gut feels as opposed to what your head says.

Bear in mind that there is a difference between the two. This is the nonverbal information which you perceive through images and not by logic. If you truly want to understand a person, what really counts is who they are inside and not their outward appearance. Your intuition enables you to unravel the depth to a person one which others may not be able to easily see. This is your gift, after all.

Checklist of Intuitive Cues

Trust your gut feeling. When it comes to first meetings, listening to your gut is key given your gift of being able to feel people's energy. For most empaths, a first meeting is more than enough for them to be able to tell if they would be able to comfortably spend time with a person or not.

In fact, some of them can have a visceral reaction to negativity, allowing them to steer away from a potentially harmful friendship. So, listen to your gut feel as this serves as your internal truth meter.

Pay attention to how your body reacts to certain interactions. In particular, observe whenever your goosebumps rise up. These are physical manifestations of energy and can be great intuitive signals that can convey information when it comes to how people move us. They tend to happen during moments of some importance, whether we realize it or not, so be more aware of their appearances.

Have you ever had an "aha!" moment? Now, for most people, they may dismiss this as nothing of value, but for empaths pay more attention whenever this happens. These are moments that could provide you with great insight into the person you're speaking to or simply the current environment you are in. These things tend to happen in a flash, however, so if you're not very alert then you can easily miss it.

As mentioned earlier, some empaths are actually capable of physically feeling another person's symptoms and emotions. Think about it, whilst you're reading people, have you ever had stabbing pain somewhere in your body?

Did a meeting with someone leave you with a tingle and an unshakable positive feeling? Speak to the person you're with, ask them if they're feeling any pain this is how you'll be able to confirm if this is a result of your empathy or something else entirely.

Sense Emotional Energy

Emotions are an expression of our overall energy. This is the vibe we give off to other people and the same ones they project onto us. Have you encountered people who simply feel really good to be around with? The energy they give off is full of vitality and they can easily improve your mood.

On the other hand, you have others who can be draining and make you want to move away from them. As subtle as these energy projections are, empaths can easily pick up on them given their inherent sensitivity to it.

Always Ask For A Workplace Tour Before Accepting A Role

When you go for an interview, ask whether you can take a tour if someone hasn't already offered to show you around. Pay attention to the employees' facial expressions, their body language, and the way they talk to one another. You'll quickly surmise whether the organization is toxic. Unless you are in desperate need of money, follow your gut instinct and avoid workplaces that contain a significant amount of negative energy.

Pay close attention to the lighting, the noise levels, the amount of clutter, and the layout of the desks. Ask yourself whether you could be comfortable working in such an environment, from both a physical and emotional perspective. A high salary might be enticing, but your health and sanity must come first. Even if other people tell you that a job is too good an opportunity to pass up, trust your intuition.

You have the power to make a positive difference in the workplace, but you are under no obligation to sacrifice your mental and physical health if doing so is beyond your comfort zone. Never feel bad about choosing the right job for you.

Use Your Gift As A Selling Point

Empaths are not show-offs by nature, and the prospect of selling yourself in a job interview might be enough to make you feel queasy. But think of it this way – your empathic qualities are actually an increasingly valuable commodity in the workplace. We tend to associate the business world, and even the public sector, with a kind of cut-throat mentality where everyone is trying to outdo one another and compete for the best positions and the most money.

However, our society is increasingly aware that taking care of one another and our planet is the only way forward. We still have a long way to go in creating a more caring world but, in general, we are starting to understand the benefit of a healthy work-life balance and the merit of cooperative working practices rather than a dog-eat-dog mentality. If you feel up to the challenge, you can use your gift to help drive this change!

You know that there is far more to life – and work – than status or salary. Your gift makes you perfectly suited to roles that require listening, conflict resolution, and mentoring skills. Psychiatrist, author, and empath Dr. Judith Orloff maintains that empaths bring passion, excellent communication skills, and leadership ability to their professional roles. When an interviewer asks what you can bring to a job, don't hesitate to give examples of times you have demonstrated these gifts.

Working Alone Versus Working With Others

Although you have strong leadership potential, a role involving extensive contact with colleagues and customers on a day-to-day basis may prove too draining, especially if you are not yet confident in your ability to handle negative energy and toxic individuals. Be honest with yourself when applying for a position. If it entails working as part of a busy team with few opportunities to recharge during the day, think carefully before making an application.

Most empaths are well suited to working for themselves or taking on jobs within small organizations. Working in a large office or noisy environment may be too stimulating – and that's fine! We all have different needs and talents, so do not allow anyone to make you feel inferior for not being able to handle a "normal" workplace. As an empath, you may quickly become overwhelmed by the prospect of having to interact with coworkers, members of the management team, and customers.

On the other hand, working alone can result in social isolation if you take it to extremes. If you decide to run a small business from home, for example, be sure to schedule some time with family and friends at least a couple of times per week.

Not only do you need to nurture your relationships, but it is also helpful to gain an outsider's perspective on your work from time to time. Sometimes, you may get so caught up in a project that relatively minor problems seem to take on a life of their own. Talking to other people allows you to take a more realistic view and help you come up with new solutions.

If Your Environment Drains Your Energy, Ask For Reasonable Adjustments

You can't expect your boss to redecorate the office just to suit your preferences or to fire an energy vampire, but you can ask them politely whether they would mind making a few small adjustments. For example, if there is a harsh strip light directly over your desk, you could ask whether it would be possible to turn off the light and use softer, gentler lamps instead.

If you work in an environment in which people talk loudly, experiment with white noise or other sound recordings designed to trigger feelings of calm and emotional stability. Try sounds recorded in nature, as these are often soothing for empaths. You can find lots of free resources on YouTube or specialized noise-generating sites such as mynoise.net. If possible, listen to natural or white noise via noise-cancellation headphones for at least a portion of your workday.

There are also additions and adjustments you can make that do not require permission from your boss. For instance, you can place crystals on your desk as a means of countering negative energy and set aside a few minutes each day – even if you are incredibly busy – to ensure your desk is clear of unnecessary clutter. If you work with a computer, pick a calming scene or color as your desktop wallpaper. Frame a photo or uplifting picture and keep it on your desk. Look at it for a few seconds when you need a dose of positive energy.

If you enjoy your job but would prefer to spend less time around other people, consider asking your manager whether you can work from home a couple of days each week. This can give you some respite from other peoples' energy and enables you to take a break at any time. Working from home comes with the privilege of setting up an environment that suits you perfectly. For example, you could install a water feature on your desk or play natural background noise throughout the day without fear of eliciting annoying questions from your coworkers.

Watch Out For Energy Vampires

If you come across an energy vampire in your personal life, you usually have the option of cutting contact with them, or at least limiting how much time the two of you spend hanging out. Unfortunately, this isn't the case when you are forced to work alongside them.

This is where boundaries come into play. You need to politely but firmly assert yourself from the outset of your professional relationship. Don't be drawn into petty workplace gossip, and don't accept any invitations from toxic people to socialize outside of work. Draw on your best energy self-defense skills, and always put your wellbeing before professional obligations.

Empaths who choose to work in the helping professions, whether with other people or animals, need to remain aware of the effect of their work on their energy levels. For example, if you work as a psychologist or therapist, speaking to a client who is going through an especially sad or difficult time in their life can leave you exhausted, depleted, and even depressed. Be sure to allow a few minutes between clients or appointments in which to ground yourself, and schedule plenty of time to relax and nurture yourself outside of work.

Draw A Line Between Your Workplace and Home

If you work outside the home, it's a good idea to devise a routine that creates a clear dividing line between your professional and personal life. As an empath, you are susceptible to carrying the negative energy of others with you. You may catch yourself worrying not only about the problems you are facing at work, but also those of your colleagues, bosses, and customers. Unless you learn how to "switch off," you will soon become overwhelmed, anxious, and depressed.

When it's time to wrap up your work for the day, stay mindful of the transition between work and home. Create a ritual that automatically encourages you to switch your focus to personal interests and feelings rather than those of colleagues and clients. For example, you may wish to spend the final five minutes of your workday in meditation or tidying your desk whilst listening to a particular soundtrack or piece of music. If you have a friend or relative who always raises your energy levels, you could get into the habit of texting them just before leaving work or on the way home.

Focus On How Your Work Helps Others

It isn't always possible to change your job or work in the field of your choosing. If you are stuck in a job that isn't right for you and are in no position to make a change any time soon, try approaching your work with a new mindset.

As an empath, you have a talent for helping others. Not only do they benefit from your support, but you also get to soak up their positive energy too. It's truly a win-win situation! Try to find opportunities to lend a hand to someone else, and offer emotional support as long as it doesn't leave you feeling too drained.

For example, if one of your colleagues seems especially stressed, take the initiative and ask them if they'd like to talk to you for five minutes about anything that's bothering them. Sometimes, just offering a listening ear can turn someone's day around! Or perhaps you could offer a more practical form of help. For instance, you could offer to take everyone's mail to the mailroom on your coffee break. Acts of service and kindness allow you to find a sense of meaning in your work, even if you are hoping to change careers in the near future.

Chapter 7 Increase the effects of communication with people

Can you imagine a world without empathy? Well, I definitely cannot because empathy is something that keeps love and compassion alive. Anyone who is hurt, broken or vulnerable needs someone who can empathize with them. If you pay attention to most relationships between couples or even between families, maximum problems arise because there is a lack of empathy.

Empaths know how to tune into the actual feelings of the person that is present beneath the outer façade. This is something that non-empaths cannot do. Empaths can open up to their gut feelings. They constantly keep asking themselves at every point in their life – 'what would I have felt if I was in the shoes of that person?'

But if you are finding it difficult to tune into others or simply want to know how this is done, then here are a set of questions that you must ask.

Am I Paying Full Attention?

If you want to understand someone's emotions properly, then paying attention to what they are saying is the first thing to do. But the entire process of communicating with someone involves three different things – listening, thinking, and speaking. So, it is a dynamic process and you can communicate on a deeper level only when you maintain a proper balance between all three of these things. The conversation also differs from person to person. For example, if you are having a conversation with someone in your family or an old friend, then the primary habit of any individual is to complete each other's' sentences. But this is exactly what causes a lot of problems. When you do not let the other person complete their own sentence, you are forgetting the basic rules of a conversation when it comes to listening.

If you want to judge yourself as to how good of a listener you are, there are many things to consider. For this, you do not necessarily have to record your conversation. All you have to do is once the conversation is over, play it over in your head. When you keep doing this from time to time, you will be noticing some patterns. Now once you notice your behavioral patterns, you need to ask yourself how much these behaviors affect your interaction with the person. For example, you might have a habit of checking your phone in between a conversation. This is a habit that will definitely affect your communication depth with the person. So, make sure you implement the changes and then you will see that you have automatically learned to communicate with others in a better way.

Are Your Multi-Tasking?

Have you ever spoken to someone while you were multi-tasking? If you have, then you probably know that any communication that was done while you were multitasking doesn't have any meaning.

When your brain is handling so many things at once, it can never concentrate on any one thing. It might even happen that you have no idea what the person just told you because you were not paying complete attention. With the advent of technology, people have increased their habit of multi-tasking but this has only decreased the quality of conversations. You, as humans, can never do multiple tasks at a time with equal efficiency.

This is because when you are multi-tasking, you are constantly switching your attention from one thing to the other. But the key to communication is placing a complete focus on the person in front of you. When you do not do that, you might misunderstand the meaning of what the person has just said or you can even miss out on a considerable portion of the conversation. Moreover, this will also slow down your brain and your brain will not be able to process the information it has just received and this includes the proper interpretation of feelings as well.

Did You Ever Check How Your Actions Are Affecting the Person in Front of You?

Tuning in to others' feelings is only possible when you make the conversation in the right way. An important part of that is checking what impact your actions are placing on the person you are talking to. This also includes your style of conversation. People usually think that a person's conversation style is influenced by their character and personality but on contrary to this belief, it is actually influenced by a lot of other factors as well.

For example, their choices, upbringing and also the experiences they received in life. The way a person communicated is their own choice.

But many a time a person does not really keep a check on how he/she is behaving during a conversation and this is also influenced by their emotions. Empaths become so concerned about the intent of delivery that they forget to notice how they have chosen to deliver the message. For example, did you notice what your facial expressions were the last time you spoke with someone? Most of you would answer no as these things are quite difficult to self-monitor. But if you truly want to tune into someone else's feelings then you need to understand the impact of your communication style and how you can improve it for the better.

Are Your Listening with the Intent to Understand?

You can learn a lot of things about a person if you listen to what they have to say. But you have to listen with the intent to understand. Every one of you must be guilty of not listening to someone actively at least once in your life. I know I am and I am not saying that you must be loathing yourself because of that. But if you want to tune into others, then listening very carefully is something you have to master. Yes, there have been moments in everyone's life when they have just nodded and smiled just at the right time and everyone thought that you were actually listening when you were not. You might have been thinking about going shopping or having that pizza after you got back home.

But have you ever been on the receiving end of the exact same situation? Do you remember how you felt? Annoyed? Neglected? Unimportant? Chances are that you felt all of the above. So, now you know why you should be paying careful attention to the person you are talking to if you truly want to understand him/her and tune into their feelings.

Being an empath is not about talking to someone just because that person wanted to tell you something. There is nothing superficial about being an empath. So, if you want to tune into others, you need to ask yourself the above three questions. After that, you also need to rid yourself of all the prejudices or premature conclusions that you might have fixated in your mind. These will only cloud your vision and you will not be able to see the actual picture.

Another thing that you have to master if you want to read their thoughts is that you have to notice the physical movements of the person you are talking to. Does the person have his/her hands or legs in a crossed position? This is often seen in people who have come up to you with a self-protective, defensive, or angry mental setting. Is the person in front of you biting his/her lips? This action usually signifies that the person is feeling awkward or is under an intense level of pressure.

You should also learn how you can interpret the facial expression of a person correctly. Emotions of a person are usually etched prominently on their faces with the help of subtle signs. All you need to do is identify those signs. When you notice deep frown lines on the forehead of a person, it usually means that the person is worrying intensely about something. When a person is quite tensed, you will notice him/her clenching their jaws or teeth. Anger or bitterness is usually signified by pursed lips. Similarly, there are several other such small things that denote a person's emotions.

Lastly, you should never ignore your gut feelings. Empaths often have very true gut feelings. Moreover, the emotions of a person have an energy of their own. So, you need to look out for that energy or vibe. If the person has positive emotions, then you will feel good to be around that person. On the contrary, if a person is full of negativity, then you will not prefer to be around that person. You will have an instant feel or instinct to leave that person then and there. Don't do anything that you feel like not doing because this will affect your emotional and mental health. Tune into those people who you feel comfortable with. Forcing yourself to tune into someone will only hamper your internal balance.

Chapter 8 Techniques of improve your persuasion skills even if you are a beginner

If you want to achieve serenity in life, then you will have to put enough effort into it as well. Just like you have to maintain a proper diet and exercise regime to get into shape, you need to build some good habits if you want to achieve peace of mind. For some reason, everyone thinks that serenity is something that can only be achieved by yoga instructors and monks. But is that the truth? Of course, not! Anyone can achieve serenity by following the right path. When you attain serenity, you will be able to enjoy life in a much better way.

Attaining peace of mind and happiness in life is essential for empaths because of their nature of absorbing others' emotions. If you keep getting engrossed in the negative energies of others, you will stop enjoying this beautiful life. But when you attain serenity, your problems will no longer seem bigger than they really are and you will stop heightening every feeling that you get. And when you face some real crises, you will be able to maintain your calm and deal with it properly. Here are some ways which can help you find serenity and give the key to a happier life.

Say Thanks for The Things You Have

If you want to achieve serenity in your life, practicing gratitude will take you a long way. Hustling towards your goal is all fine but will that make you happy at the end of the day? Not always. But what will make you feel happy is if you think about all the things you have and how blessed you are to have them. The moment you start practicing contentment in your life, practicing gratitude will become way easier. You will feel thankful for all that you have the moment you train yourself to become content with what you have achieved in life. Accept yourself the way you are and learn to let go of perfectionism.

Stop fretting over the things that happened in the past because that will be of no use. What has happened has already happened and there is nothing you can do about it. So, you need to start living in your present. Focus on those small joys in your everyday life. Another way of ensuring a greater sense of gratitude in life is to offer moral support to others in need. But since you are an empath, you should be careful about not absorbing all their emotions. All you need to do is listen to them. You also need to stop overthinking about your future. No matter how many plans you make, life will happen. Don't spend hours thinking about that dream home because it doesn't really matter now. Revel in your present and think how blessed you are to have all that you currently possess.

Learn to Accept

Some people interpret acceptance to be something it is not. You need to understand that practicing acceptance does not mean that you have to endure every injustice that is being done to you. If you are being poorly treated by someone then that is not the place for acceptance. Acceptance means that you need to learn how to accept people the way they are without wanting to change them at all. If someone in your life is a jerk, then you need to accept the fact that it is in their nature. But it will always be in your hands whether you want to spend time with them or not. The thing that you have to accept is that you can't really change people.

One the other hand, implementing acceptance in your life does not mean you will not find any room for improvement. Read this example and you should understand the concept better. You might be living in an apartment that you are not quite happy about. But you can't just go out of your house and start living somewhere else, right? First, you need to see whether you can afford your dream house or not. And if you cannot afford it right now, then the best way to deal with it is to accept your situation for now and continue living in your old house. At the same time, figure out ways in which you can save money for your dream house so that one day you can move in there.

Keep Your Mind on the Right Track

Your mind can get off track from time to time and that is completely normal. Do you find yourself getting frustrated over very small things in life? Do you find yourself imagining that it is always your job to fix someone's behavior if you think it is not right? Well, if you are someone who does all these things, then your mind is definitely going off its course at times but you can also bring it back on track with a little bit of practice. The moment you find your mind going in the wrong lane, you need to stop it then and there.

If you find that someone is not behaving properly, you might feel that you are obliged to help him/her just because you are an empath. This is not true. If you want to find serenity then the right way would be to move away from that person. Then, engage in any activity that you think might help you to get yourself back on the right course. It can be something like listening to music or it can also be talking to your best friend. When you start re-directing your mind, your focus will no more be clouded by other things and you can think with clarity.

Make Amends

Do you think you have treated someone unkindly? Don't sleep over it as some might suggest. The moment you ignore your guilt, it will start accumulating in your subconscious mind. So, you need to accept the fact that you have treated someone in a way you shouldn't have and you also need to take proper measures to make amends. Moreover, try to make amends as soon as you can because this will help to keep the guilt at bay.

If you keep the guilt buried in your heart for a long time, it will take a toll on you. They can even fuel negative energies and cause you to be in denial. Sometimes, people get into a vicious cycle and instead of making amends, put the blame on others. This is an example of a self-destructive attitude. There is nothing wrong with apologizing and coming clean about what you have done because it will help you clear your conscience. It will also assist you in repairing your broken relationships. The first step to making amends is to forgive yourself for what you have done. If you are not able to do that, you will not be able to ask for forgiveness from someone else as well.

Be Kind

In no possible situation can an unkind behavior benefit you. You must be extra careful about how you are behaving because this will also have a direct impact on your mood. This is even truer for empaths. When you say or do something bad to someone, it affects them adversely and if you are an empath, then you will pick up the feeling or emotion of the person in front of you and start feeling the exact same pain they felt. So, whenever you are hurting someone in front of you, you are also hurting yourself indirectly. If you are experiencing this in your life, then it is time that you take a long hard look at yourself and what you are doing and analyze your actions.

Be kind to everyone consistently. Help them overcome their sorrows in life. Build their confidence levels. When you are kind to someone, you will see that you are making a social connection with that person. You will automatically have an improved mood when you help someone. You can also try volunteering at various camps. Moreover, kindness always comes back around in some way or the other. If you are kind to others, the world will be kind to you as well.

Clean Your Home

Have you ever noticed any dirty towels or dirty floors in any spa? I'm sure your answer will be no because there is a psychological connection between staying clean and staying happy. If your place is messy, you cannot relax there because there is a lot of pent up energy in the room that you, as an empath, can feel. Moreover, it is said that whenever someone has a cluttered room, it directly portrays their state of mind which is also in a state of chaos. So, you need to make your room or your house clean.

The moment you clean away the mess, you will be able to de-stress. Empaths become exhausted from bearing all those emotions in a day and if you come back to a house that is messy and full of things lying around here and there, your mind will not be able to attain the peace it wants. You don't need to burn yourself out by trying to clean the entire house in a day. You can start by cleaning one room or one portion of a house in a day and by the end of the week, your house will become all sorted. Keeping your bedroom clean should be your first priority because that is where you come at the end of the day to crash. So, a better idea would be to start the cleaning from your bedroom itself.

Mix with the Right Kind of People

Everyone has some people in their life who are of no support but rather a problem. They always carry some drama with them wherever they go. They are always upset about something or the other in their life because someone has broken their heart or someone has said something insulting. Or probably these people simply can't say anything nice to you. These people can leave a very bad emotional impact on empaths. There are some people with whom you can stop mixing with but there will always be some who cannot be eliminated.

In that case, you can try and limit your exposure to such kind of toxic people. There is nothing to feel bad about it because it will be for your own good. It will be the right step towards attaining serenity and happiness and thus a matter of self-preservation. When there is chaos in your life, you cannot concentrate on anything else and doing things for your own happiness starts seeming like a far-fetched concept. You have to remember that even though you are an empath, it is not your job to solve others' problems or to make them feel better. When you spend time with people who motivate you, you will automatically feel more energized and you will always be in the right mood.

Get Exposed to the Right Kind of Media

The different kind of media that you get exposed to in a day plays a huge role in your life too. This includes the TV shows you watch, the movies you see on Netflix or any other web platform or the books you read. All of these leave a mark on your thinking process. If there is a certain type of genre that you love specifically, it doesn't mean that you have to watch everything in that genre. Filter what you watch or read. Sometimes, these media will impart pointless junk that can influence you negatively. If something is too strenuous for you mentally, don't watch just because your friends asked you to.

Watch or read things that make you feel happy or interest you. Don't get involved with media that invokes fear or negative thinking or puts you in a situation of self-doubt. When you watch or read something that imparts a positive vibe, you can benefit from it in numerous ways. If you have free time in your day, why waste it by filling it with garbage when there are so many helpful and uplifting contents out there? It is better to not watch anything than to watch something that demotivates you.

Validate Yourself

Do you want to experience peace in your life? Well, the first step to peace is self-validation. The most common misconception about the concept of validation that everyone has is that they believe it somehow means that you agree or approve of something. But this is not how self-validation works. Instead, it is about acceptance of the internal experience of a human being. It has nothing to do with the justification of the person's thoughts or feelings. Many a time in your life, you will find thoughts cropping up in your mind that you don't fully agree with. You will know it in your heart that the thoughts that you are having are not justified in any way. But judging yourself for having these thoughts or being hard on yourself will only cause a toll on you emotionally and you might also miss out on some important information.

But, if you practice self-validation, then you will be looking for ways in which you can stay calm and at the same time, manage the situation more effectively. You will see that you have started to understand yourself in a better way and this, in turn, will help build a strong identity. You will also improve when it comes to handling intense emotions in life. This is often difficult for empaths but once you start validating yourself, even this should seem easier. You will find wisdom through the process of self-validation. Another thing that you should keep in mind is that validation and mindfulness are two very related things and they often go hand in hand.

Accurate reflection of your current predicament is a very crucial part of self-validation. You need to label your internal state of mind accurately to validate yourself in the right manner. You also need to start normalizing your emotions. Empaths tend to think that whatever intense emotions they are feeling are not normal. But everyone has their own emotions and having them at intense levels is also completely normal. Never lie to yourself about anything and stay true to yourself. This means that you should never be an imposter or try to be someone you are not. Being in denial of who you are as a person is one of the biggest reasons why people invalidate themselves. So, in case you are facing this, you need to start accepting yourself right from today. You also need to realize that what you do does not define who you are as a person. But yes, in case changing some of your behaviors for the positive alleviated your pains then you can do so.

Self-validation is a process and it will not happen in a day. The more you practice, the better you will get at it. So, don't leave hope and love yourself a bit more every day.

Chapter 9 Application in the Real World

The concept of empathy can be difficult to grasp as anything other than just that; an abstract concept. So, try and incorporate the things you've learned while reading this book into situations you see in your everyday life. That may mean being aware of yourself if and when you have an angry outburst and being able to quickly and calmly diffuse the situation before having to wait for someone else to. It might also mean knowing what to do when you find yourself in a crowded area and are feeling panicked or trapped; suffering from sensory overload, but calm and knowledgeable enough to know how to remove yourself from that bad situation and whom to talk to about it afterward. These are only a few of the situations that you are now infinitely more prepared for by learning about empaths, and hopefully, learning about yourself as well.

Now that you have a much better grasp on the abstract concepts that come with being an empath, as well as coping with and moving past all the obstacles that may ensue, it's time to take a closer look at how exactly to apply everything you've learned to a real-life scenario. We've already discussed emotional intelligence and what to do when put in a situation where someone you know is either an empath who is suffering from a bad period, or who do not have the emotional intelligence to communicate what exactly they want from you to you. In general, here are some rules of thumb, both for empaths struggling to make their lives easier, and for those who have someone close to them who is an empath who might be struggling to reach his or her most organic, authentic self:

Validation is so, so important. Verifying the feelings of an empath, or having your feeling verified as an empath, can be one of the most emotionally uplifting and healing things someone can hear, even if it is only a temporary euphoria.

If you're someone with a highly sensitive loved one, check up on them. Not only will this ensure that they at least know someone is there who will do this for them relatively often, but the small gesture will never be lost on an empath. Additionally, from the point of view of an empath, don't be afraid to ask things like that of the people around you! There are infinitely many people around you who can love and support you through anything and everything, but no one can know what you want out of them if you don't take the leap of faith and ask. The worst that can result from this is the person turning you down. In this case, it may be that this person not only a very good part of your support system, to begin with, but they may also be an extra source of your stress that you certainly don't need to add to any of your lists. It's their loss, not yours.

Don't ever be afraid to ask for help—not only does this go for loved ones, and your personal support system, but outside sources of help as well! Whether it be that you're seeking out medication, or simply think that you would feel much better or more support if you could discuss your emotional pain with someone who is not only licensed but is an experienced professional who will know how to help you in the most truly straightforward and effective way possible. Asking for help does not make you weak, it makes you much stronger and much, much braver than you might realize.

Be proud of what you've accomplished so far—even if it doesn't seem like you've done much for yourself quite yet, be proud of all the baby steps, all the very first steps you've taken in the direction you know is the right one.

Humanize yourself—we, as humans, far too often get stuck in a storybook narrative: we want so desperately to be special and undeniably unique that we don't see the unique and indispensable qualities about ourselves when we look in the mirror! Never forget that treating yourself like nothing more than an archetype might feel nice at the moment, but labeling yourself as a static character does nothing but harm your sense of personality, sense of belonging, and sense of self. You don't need to be the protagonist of a fantasy realm to be the main character of your own story! While on this subject, remember that the people you interact with every day may be secondary characters, your partners in crime or they may be simply recurring extras in your metaphorical story. You are the only main character, the only true protagonist of your story. Use this to your advantage! There can be a strong sense of confidence that comes from the knowledge that no one can outshine you on your own stage. Know that no one else can replace your spotlight, no matter how important they may seem in the moment, no matter how long they stay in your story, it will always and forever be your story and your story alone. Only you have the power to change it.

Be open and honest with yourself. This might be one of the most difficult things on this list to do, especially as a highly sensitive person. You, as an empath, are vulnerable to very slight shifts in energy. When the energy of a person changes, especially yourself, you feel the weight of that change fully and bluntly. So, when you do sense a change, own up to it and admit it. We have a tendency to act as nothing has changed in situations where something has very obviously changed in the hopes that if we don't acknowledge change, it won't come to pass. This isn't the case, of course, so we need to own up to it and be upfront with ourselves and our loved ones. Communication is the key between you and your support system! If you feel like something has shifted and you don't like it, talk to someone you trust about it. If this doesn't satisfy you, talk to a therapist about the changed going on in your life. Being honest and as authentic as you possibly can be to everyone around you will ease the pain that this change might have brought on you and your loved ones. Being honest and authentic is also an important step toward harnessing your abilities and making your empathy your tool to control, not a tool which controls you. Being especially honest with yourself, especially when the truth is uncomfortable, is very hard, but it's something that has to be done. Be proud of yourself afterward for having the strength to be totally honest, real, and authentic. You're making a lot of progress.

Be sure to make plenty of mistakes. Mistakes are so, unendingly important. Understanding what it means to make a mistake is understanding what it means to not be perfect, something everyone, especially empaths, will have to learn for themselves eventually. It also means learning what it means to learn; most of the learning process is made up of mistakes. You start, mess up, start over a little better, mess up again, and so on and so forth. You mess up as many times as you can possibly count and beyond, and you will have a finished product that is several times better than the final product of someone that did it perfectly the first try. You took the time to learn about the process and internalize what you did wrong, understand why it was wrong and improved upon it. The same can be applied to your personal life, your relationships, and yourself as a whole, as an empath. You will certainly mess up while you're communicating and learning about your abilities. This doesn't mean the final product won't be magnificent! It just means that your final product of an amazing and functional empath will take more time, more care, love, compassion, and support to be fostered into an adult who understands their place in the world and knows how to get what they want using their abilities. Your support system will understand that you are going through a phase of trial and error where you are trying to find out what exactly works for you, and that's fine. It's a part of you, and the people who love you the most will wait for you to come out of your shell and become the best version of yourself. They love you, and they won't leave you just because you make a mistake or two. So, have fun with your mistakes! Make as many as you want, because the process of finding out who you are may be your only chance to recklessly make mistakes and love it.

Perhaps the most important part of applying what you've learned throughout this book to the real world is loving yourself. It's hard; very, very, very hard. But you can do it. Everyone believes in you. Keep working at it for as long as you can, because loving yourself is a tall order. Especially of an empath, and especially in today's society where we're pressured to only love ourselves if we look and act a certain way. Chances are that loving yourself is even harder than learning how to function in the world as an empath, regardless of your past and of what type you are. Learning to love yourself opens up every opportunity in the world to you and only you. Being able to see yourself the way the people who love you the most see you are a wonderful gift, one that is a hard-earned privilege to have. Not only is it incredibly difficult to love what you criticize in the mirror every day, but it's also hard to keep it up. You'll stumble sometimes, and feel like giving up. Everyone has days where they want to give up. What makes a truly powerful person is whether or not they actually listen to the voice in the back of their head that keeps telling them to lie down and give up. So, get back up. Your loved ones will help you. Your family, whether it's the one you were given at birth or the one you found on your own, will help you. You're not alone in anything you do. You have the support of so many people by your side. Get back up, and try again, and love yourself.

Keeping the above and any other information that may have stuck out to you over the course of this book in mind, tread forward! The road ahead of you may seem terrifying and uncertain, but as long as you keep moving forward, you will reach the end of the rainbow and emerge a happier and overall better version of yourself. Of course, remember that although you have to move forward to reach your end goal of a happier you who can harness your feelings and use them for good to yourself and to others, you will not always feel like you are moving forward. Some days, you will likely even feel that you are moving in the exact opposite direction, drifting further and further away from your goal. As you heal, you will encounter all sorts of negative emotions, bad days, and many other sorts of negative influences in your life. Know that none of these things are permanent—they are negative, but they are ultimately fleeting things. As you heal more and more by weeks, by months, and by years, you will find that you have less and less bad days and more and more good ones.

That perseverance, over weeks, months, and many years, will serve you well when you can look back on your life and definitively decide that you've led a successful and productive life as an empath. The satisfaction that comes with knowing that you've overcome your fears and learned how to harness your abilities and gifts that come with being highly sensitive cannot be paralleled.

Conclusion

The next step is to start experimenting with various healing methods in order to find one—or several, if you're lucky—that address your needs. It is always advisable to experience any healing practice from the standpoint of a patient, client, or student before jumping into a training program or offering yourself as a healer. It is also wise to focus on connecting with as many other empaths and alternative healers as you can find, both socially and professionally. There may not be many fellow empaths in your immediate social or professional circles, but I assure you, like-minded spirits are out there, and they are eager to receive and connect with you! Browse online forums, podcasts, and social media platforms; seek out retreats, or find an inclusive spiritual organization in your area; yoga classes attract empaths like moths to a flame. It may take some effort, but once you start to keep an eye out for fellow empaths, you may be pleasantly surprised to find that we are everywhere, and we all want to support your journey to become a healer.

When empaths come together, their combined strength is multiplied exponentially. Though we are gaining recognition in the fields of psychology and science, we still are a minority in the world. We must support each other, empower each other, share our personal stories, and teach each other, to ensure that the light of empathy continues to spread and grow brighter with every passing year.

CPSIA information can be obtained
at www.ICGtesting.com
Printed in the USA
BVHW090205250621
610375BV00001B/224